COOKING SIMPLE
with
Sheila Rae

Sheila Rae, LLC

Enjoy the Art of Cooking Simple! Sheila Rae

COOKING SIMPLE
with
Sheila Rae

Copyright © 2004

1st printing   November 2004

For ordering information
go to
Sheilaraellc.com

Wimmer Cookbooks

Acknowledgements

Welcome to *Cooking Simple with Sheila Rae*. This book is written for the person who would love to impress friends and family without the hassle of those long and drawn-out recipes. As a Home Economics teacher for 11 years, I learned to make the complicated into the simple, and that is exactly what this collection of recipes is—simple. Please take the time to read the front of this book as well as all the helpful hints throughout, they will make your time in the kitchen much more enjoyable.

This book is dedicated to some incredible people who have a lot of faith in me: my husband, Erik; my two wonderful children, Zach and Elizabeth; my parents, Bill and Marlene; and Erik's mother, Lyla. My family is so large that to name them all would take a page by itself, because as Erik and I have moved around the country, we have developed such wonderful relationships with people whom we consider family.

A special thanks to Jerry and Faith McCollough for the wonderful artwork shown in this book.

Flexipans® : Flexible Bakeware by Demarle

I found these pans about four years ago after seeing them on the cooking network. I ordered the muffin mold from France and fell in love. In 2003, I discovered that they were being sold in the United States. Instantly my Demarle collection grew, and other pans that I had acquired over the years started leaving my home. Not because the old pans were ineffective, but because the clean up of a metal or glass baking dish is very time consuming, and I have a hate-hate relationship with non-stick spray coatings. They get everywhere, and frankly I don't need the extra calories or hassles.

I would like to teach you about these amazing products that are going to revolutionize the American market. This product is durable, flexible, and versatile, and cleans with a swish in hot soapy water. The material is black and made of silicone and woven glass. It can withstand temperatures of 480 degrees; plus it can withstand freezer temperature and is microwave safe. These Flexipans® eliminate the need for multiple pans and create attractive food at the same time. I often stir mixes (such as cakes) directly in these pans before baking, which leaves only the one pan to clean!

Over the past four years I have shared these amazing pans with people with such joy and excitement. Seeing their delighted faces as I easily invert sticky, cheesy or frozen items onto serving trays gives me so much pleasure.

Note: Imitation pans have entered the market, but BEWARE! They do not work the same, because they are solid silicone, which is by nature totally heat resistant. I cannot figure out why anyone would want to bake in a heat resistant pan. You'll often find hot pads of the same material and design in the same shelf display. This does not speak well for their other products.

Another product that I love in the kitchen is dental floss (yes, you can use mint). I use dental floss to even out cakes and cut dough, sandwiches, and cakes. Floss is tough and inexpensive; I keep a container in my kitchen.

Beware! There are a lot of "beautiful' tools, but some are not accurate and accuracy and good cooking go hand-in-hand.

If you need help just email and I will give you pointers on any of the recipes. When we created this book we wanted our customers to be able to ask questions and connect with the author.

Sheilaraellc.com

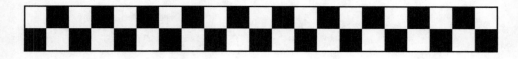

Tips:

Replace baking powder and soda at least every year. They do go bad and can affect the quality of the food. I pour them down the sink with running water-a great cleaner.

Buy the best that you can afford when it comes to chocolate, wine, syrups, flavorings and spices. Watch for expiration dates. Always buy real vanilla extract. Imitation needs to stay in its container, and is best left there.

Cake Mixes:
1.   Watch expiration dates.
2.   I love cake mixes for their convenience. I have discovered through a friend to stir the cake mix up and let it sit in the bowl for 20 minutes; stir it one more time, and pour it in the pan, and bake. The artificial flavor is GONE. Amazing!

Chocolate:
1.   Buy the best.
2.   Look for high lecithin, or wax contents. Leave them in the store.
3.   When melting, heat whatever it is to which the chocolate will be added, then add the chocolate. This process prevents ceasing and burning.

      "Ceasing" means that chocolate becomes hard, and you have to try to re-temper it, or break it up and use it in chocolate chip cookies.

Bread:
Bread is easy once you have the basics. Check out the Simple Sheila Rae Bread Recipe for wonderful hints.

Quick Breads:
Mix the dry ingredients in one bowl and liquid ingredients in another, and then mix them together. DO NOT OVER STIR. Quick breads are very sensitive and are one of the last items I mastered to my satisfaction. I have discovered that when I ignore the more complicated instructions and instead follow my simple tip, all quick bread recipes work out much better.

Party Planning:
The best hint for parties is: NEVER tell what you are making. Give people only the necessary information. I believe this is the best tip is because if something does not work out, no one else will know; that in turn reduces your stress.

Salt:
Salt is a very important staple in the American kitchen but I would like to share some tips about buying the right salt.

Sea salt is my favorite it is all natural and truly adds a wonderful accent to food without being overpowering.

Kosher salt can be used for all purposes from salting water for pasta to baking. I do prefer it over Iodized salt. I feel Iodized salt has too harsh of flavor and can become over powering.

Calorie Conscience tips to live HEALTHIER BY:

1. Use more flavors by adding spices, vinegar and wines.

    Example: Balsamic vinegar is fabulous with sweets.

2. Use less oil. I use yogurt whenever possible in place of oil.

3. In soups, use pureed beans instead of cream for adding protein and thickening. You can also add quick oatmeal for the last 15 minutes to thicken. My preference is to take out some liquid add the oats and cook till soft then blend into the product.

4. Use egg whites in place of egg yolks. For one large egg add 2 egg whites.

5. FORGET THE MARGARINE—just use less butter for the added flavor or natural fruit and jellies.

6. Most low fat dairy is quite good when used in recipes, but does not have the palatability of full fat products, so don't eat it plain. You will still be looking for that full body taste and end up eating something that provides it. Use evaporated skim milk in place of cream in recipes. It will save you 800 calories per cup.

7. Salad is so good but can be SO BAD. Be careful not to add heavy dressing. Use salsas for flavor and color. Salsas are NOT just tomato based they can also be fruit or other vegetables chopped with juices.

8. Rethink your pantry. Buy low-fat snacks, but remember low-fat only works if you eat only the recommended serving, which is usually only a few items. Think before you enter the check out. Do you have what you really NEED? Rethink your choices. Do you really need what is in your cart? Do you have impulse buys? Did you buy it solely because it was on sale?

9. Shop ONLY the outer edges of the grocery store. WATCH OUT FOR END CAPS— they are draws to get you to head down the aisle.

10. Watch out for the little things. Fifteen seconds of non-stick cooking spray is equal to 1 tablespoon of oil or 14 grams of fat.

11. Use olive oil instead of other oils. Extra virgin has the strongest flavor, while oil marked just "olive oil" has the least amount of olive flavor. Don't forget that you can bake with it too.

TABLE OF CONTENTS

SIMPLE BEGINNINGS

Appetizers and Beverages

Cheddar-Chili Cheesecake

¼ cup dry bread crumbs, finely ground

1¾ cups sharp Cheddar cheese, shredded

3 (8-ounce) packages cream cheese, softened

1 cup spicy sausage, fried

5 green onions, chopped

2 small jalapeño peppers, minced

1 clove garlic, minced

1 cup sour cream

2 tablespoons milk

3 large eggs

Preheat the oven to 300 degrees. Stir together bread crumbs and ¼ cup shredded cheese; sprinkle on the bottom of a 2-quart baking dish. Beat cream cheese at medium speed with an electric mixer; add sausage, 1½ shredded cheese, onions, jalapeño peppers, garlic, sour cream and milk. Beat on low speed until well blended. Add eggs and just combine; do not over beat. Pour into baking dish and bake for 1 hour or until center is set. Let stand for 30 minutes. Unmold onto a serving dish.

Serve with crackers, or warm tortilla chips.

Eggs have such an important roll in a great cheesecake. If you over whip them you will incorporate too much air and it will cause the cheesecake to rise and then fall when cool; which results in cracks.

Cheese Cups

1 ½ cups fresh Parmesan cheese, grated
½ teaspoon fresh herb
2 ½ cups fresh greens, torn
½ cup cabbage, shredded

½ cup Italian salad dressing
¼ cup olives, chopped
3 anchovies, chopped

Preheat the oven to 400 degrees. Place ½ cup of cheese and a few pieces of fresh herbs into approximately 6-inch circles on your non-stick lined baking sheet. Bake till brown. Let set 2 minutes on sheet. Carefully remove circle from pan, place hot cheese circle onto the bottom of a small bowl and let cool. Toss salad fixings and fill cups.

Cheese Wafers

1 cup butter
1 cup sharp Cheddar cheese, grated
2 cups all-purpose flour, sifted
⅛ teaspoon red pepper flakes

⅛ teaspoon garlic salt
⅛ teaspoon onion salt
¼ teaspoon Worcestershire sauce

Let butter and grated cheese stand at room temperature for an hour. Preheat oven to 375 degrees. In large mixing bowl, add the remaining ingredients; mixture will come together to form a ball as it is worked. Roll out onto large non-stick surface using a 1-inch round cookie cutter; cut out wafers. Place on non-stick lined baking sheet and bake 5 to 7 minutes, until brown.

Crabmeat Puffs

2 egg whites	1 cup crabmeat, broken apart
1 cup mayonnaise	1 pound of 1½-inch toasted bread
1 teaspoon black pepper	rounds

Preheat the oven to 375 degrees. Beat egg whites until stiff and fold in mayonnaise, pepper and crabmeat. Spoon onto bread and place on non-stick lined baking sheet. Sprinkle with paprika and broil for about 3 minutes until puffy and brown. Serve immediately.

These are wonderful with shrimp or even chicken.

Dried Beef Dip

1⅓ cups mayonnaise	2 tablespoons onion, minced
1⅓ cups sour cream	2 teaspoons parsley
2 teaspoons seasoning salt	1 (6-ounce) jar dried beef, shredded
2 teaspoons dill weed	1 (16-ounce) box of crackers

Mix mayonnaise, sour cream, salt, dill weed, onion and parsley together and add beef. Form into ball using plastic wrap. Chill. Serve with crackers.

English Muffin Salmon Puffs

1   (3-ounce) package cream cheese, softened
1   egg
½   cup Cheddar cheese, grated
¼   cup mayonnaise

1   tablespoon Worcestershire sauce
½   teaspoon dill
1   cup salmon
6   English muffins, halved

Preheat the oven to broil. Mix together cream cheese, egg, Cheddar cheese, mayonnaise, Worcestershire sauce, dill, and then add salmon. Divide mixture evenly over English muffins. Broil on non-stick lined baking sheet, until small bubbles start to appear. Cut each muffin half into quarters.

The muffins may be spread ahead of time and put in the freezer for future use.

Fruit Salsa

3   apples, coarsely chopped
2   kiwis, coarsely chopped
1   quart strawberries, coarsely chopped

2   tablespoons brown sugar
1   tablespoon lemon juice
1   tablespoon strawberry jam

Mix all the ingredients together. Refrigerate until ready to serve.

My family loves it on ice cream.

Serve with sweet chips.

Guadaloupe Salad Dressing

2	cups olive oil	3	tablespoons garlic, crushed
5	medium onions, sliced thin	1	tablespoon Italian seasonings
1	tablespoon dried rosemary	2	cups vinegar
1	teaspoon dried parsley	1½	teaspoons Kosher salt

In large saucepan sauté onions until translucent and add remaining ingredients; cook on low heat for 30 minutes. Pour into jars and refrigerate.

Anything with garlic and oil needs to be refrigerated, botulism spores will form if left on counter.

I love this dressing and we eat it on salad, fish and bread.

Hanky Panky's

1	pound hamburger	¾	teaspoon oregano
1	pound hot sausage	1	tablespoon dried onion flakes
1	pound American cheese, shredded	1	loaf party rye bread
1	teaspoon garlic salt		

Preheat the oven to 350 degrees. Brown and drain grease from meat. Add spices and cheese; stir until cheese is melted. Spread on party rye bread, place on a non-stick lined baking sheet and bake for 10 minutes or until warm.

Hot Apple Cider

1 gallon apple cider	2 cinnamon sticks
6 cups water	1 (6-ounce) can frozen orange juice
1 cup brown sugar	1 (6-ounce) can frozen lemonade
1 tablespoon pumpkin pie spice	

In a large stock pot heat all ingredients.

Lyla's Small Quiches

2 cups fresh eggs	2 tablespoons onion, minced
2 cups milk or cream	¼ cup bacon, crumbled
⅛ teaspoon pepper	¼ cup salsa
1 cup cheese, shredded	

Preheat the oven to 425 degrees. In 12 muffin tray or 20 mini-muffin tray divide bacon, cheese, salsa and onions. In mixing bowl, whisk eggs, milk and pepper; divide among muffin tin. Bake 10 minutes; turn oven down to 350 and bake an additional 10 minutes or until center is almost set, but soft. Remove from oven and let cool for 10 minutes.

I prefer these in mini-tartlet trays and I serve them at brunches.

This recipe is one that my mother-in-law Lyla loves to make when she wants to impress her guests.

Meat and Cheese Roll-Ups

1	recipe Simply Sheila Rae Bread	⅓	pound cheese	
⅓	pound meat, thinly sliced	¼	cup condiment	

Split dough into 2 batches. Roll one batch out to an approximately ¼-inch thick rectangle on a non-stick surface. Layer half of your combination on dough, leaving ½-inch empty on the top long edge. Roll into tube, cut into 1½-inch section and place on non-stick lined baking sheet. Cover and let rest 30 minutes. Preheat oven to 400 degrees. Brush with milk. Bake 10 to 12 minutes or until golden brown.

Popular combinations:

1. mayonnaise, chicken and Monterey Jack cheese
2. salsa, chicken and Monterey Jack cheese
3. horseradish sauce, seafood and Swiss cheese
4. thousand island dressing, drained sauerkraut, corn beef and Swiss cheese
5. ketchup, beef, sautéed onions and Swiss cheese
6. mustard, bologna and America cheese
7. horseradish, beef and American cheese
8. relish, chicken and sharp Cheddar
9. pizza sauce, chicken and feta cheese
10. flavored rice, meat and cheese
11. roast vegetables meat and cheese
12. pot roast, vegetables, and cheese
13. left over Chinese, Thai or Mexican food and cheese
14. broccoli, beef, teriyaki sauce and Monterey Jack cheese

I use shredded cheese in my roll-ups.

Try any combination of meat, cheese and vegetables, we have not found one we have not liked except. My friend Amy and I tried cranberries, turkey and cheese as a joke for Thanksgiving and it was hard to swallow. To this day our friend Mark and my husband Erik still laughs about that experiment.

Mexican Fudge

2 cups Monterey Jack cheese, shredded
1 cup Cheddar cheese, shredded
1 cup mozzarella cheese, shredded

3 eggs, beaten
2/3 cup salsa, drained
1 (24-ounce) bag tortilla chips

Preheat the oven to 350 degrees. Mix together half of each cheese in 1-quart baking dish. Mix together eggs and sauce; pour over cheeses and add the remaining cheese. Bake for 30 minutes. Cool completely. Invert onto serving platter; surround with chips.

Party Pizza Appetizers

1 pound hot sausage, cooked and drained
3/4 cup onion, chopped
1/4 cup black olives, chopped
1/2 cup Monterey Jack cheese, grated
1/2 cup Parmesan cheese, grated

1 1/2 teaspoons Italian seasoning
1 teaspoon garlic powder
1 (8-ounce) can tomato sauce
1 (6-ounce) can tomato paste
3 (10-ounce) cans flaky biscuits

Preheat the oven to 425 degrees. Combine sausage, onion, olives, cheeses, seasoning, garlic powder, tomato sauce and paste. Separate each biscuit into 3 parts. Spread with mixture. Bake for 10 minutes on non-stick lined baking sheet.

Pizza Cups

¾	pound ground beef	½	teaspoon salt	
2	tablespoons onion, chopped	1	teaspoon Italian seasoning	
1	teaspoon garlic, minced	1	(10-ounce) can refrigerator biscuits	
1	(6-ounce) can tomato paste	½	cup mozzarella cheese, shredded	

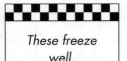

These freeze well.

Preheat the oven to 400 degrees. In a saucepan brown and drain beef and add onion, garlic, tomato paste and seasonings. Cook over low heat, stir. Place biscuits into a 12-cup muffin tray; press to cover bottom and sides. Split meat mixture evenly among holes. Sprinkle with cheese. Bake for 12 minutes or until golden brown.

Sausage Appetizers

¼	cup butter	1	egg, beaten
½	cup chicken broth	¼	pound spicy sausage
1	(6-ounce) box stuffing mix	1	pound bacon

Preheat the oven to 375 degrees. Heat butter; add broth, stuffing mix, egg and sausage. Blend with hands. Chill 1 hour. Shape into 1-inch balls. Cut bacon in thirds; wrap around balls and insert toothpicks to hold bacon in place. Bake for 35 minutes on non-stick lined baking sheet.

Strawberry Salsa

2½ cups fresh strawberries, chopped
1   kiwi, chopped
1   cup yellow pepper, chopped
2   tablespoons green onions, chopped
2   tablespoons fresh cilantro, minced

¼   cup French salad dressing
⅛   teaspoon hot pepper sauce
¼   teaspoon pepper
1   (24-ounce) bag tortilla chips

Combine together the strawberries, kiwi, yellow peppers, green onions, cilantro, salad dressing, hot pepper sauce and pepper; refrigerate for 2 hours. Serve salsa with tortilla chips.

Sweet Chips

2   (16-ounce) packages flour tortilla
⅓   cup sugar

1¼ cups cinnamon

Preheat the oven to 350 degrees. Brush or sprinkle water on each tortilla; then sprinkle with the sugar and cinnamon. Stack them and cut into ⅛'s. Place on non-stick lined baking sheet and bake for 5 to 10 minutes or until crispy.

Good warm served with fruit salsa.

These are great snacks for kids after school.

SIMPLE
ENTRÉES

Entrées

Awesome Steaks

4   (8-ounce) rib-eye steaks
2   tablespoons sea salt

¼   cup prepared horseradish sauce

Rub seasoning salt on both sides of steaks. Let rest at room temperature for 15 minutes. Heat grill. Place steaks on the grill and with a heavy tray to cover the steaks. Cook 4 minutes and turn. Cover and grill for 4 more minutes. Remove from grill and allow to rest 5 minutes before serving. Serve with sauce.

Just remember every grill is different. Four minutes on each side produces a medium done steak on my grill.

Baked Chinese Casserole

1½ pounds cooked chicken, chopped
½   cup onion, chopped
2   cups celery, chopped
1   (10¾-ounce) can chicken rice soup
1   (10¾-ounce) can cream of onion soup

6   tablespoons soy sauce
1   (8-ounce) can water chestnuts, sliced
1   (15-ounce) can chow mein vegetables
1   (10-ounce) chow mein noodles

Preheat the oven to 325 degrees. Mix all ingredients in a 3-quart baking dish. Bake for 1½ hours.

This recipe goes beautifully with steamed white rice.

Baked Macaroni

3	cups macaroni, cooked	¼	teaspoon salt
3	cups Monterey Jack cheese, grated, divided	½	teaspoon paprika
		⅛	teaspoon cayenne pepper
4	eggs	1	cup bread crumbs
2	cups milk		

Preheat the oven to 400 degrees. In a 2-quart baking dish, mix macaroni and 2⅓ cups cheese. Beat eggs, milk and seasonings and pour over macaroni and cheese. Sprinkle top with remaining cheese combined with bread crumbs. Bake for 40 minutes. Cool 5 minutes and unmold onto a tray.

My family likes when I add ham and cooked vegetables.

Baked Turkey Casserole

2	cups cooked turkey, cubed	½	teaspoon salt
1	cup celery, chopped	½	teaspoon pepper
4	teaspoons onion, diced	2	tablespoons lemon juice
4	hard-boiled eggs, chopped	½	cup margarine
⅔	cup cream of chicken soup	1	cup potato chips, crushed
½	cup almonds, slivered		

Preheat the oven to 350 degrees. Mix all the ingredients except potato chips in a 3-quart baking dish and top with chips. Bake for 30 minutes.

Barbecued Meatballs

3	pounds ground beef		2	teaspoons salt
1	(12-ounce) can evaporated milk		1	teaspoon pepper
2	cups cracker crumbs		2	teaspoons chili powder
2	eggs, beaten		4	cups ketchup
1	cup onion, chopped, divided		1	cup brown sugar
1½	teaspoons garlic powder, divided			

Preheat the oven to 350 degrees. Mix together ground beef, evaporated milk, cracker crumbs, eggs, ½ cup chopped onion, ½ teaspoon garlic powder, salt, pepper and chili powder. Form into meatballs. Place on a ¼ sheet cake pan. Bake for 20 minutes. Mix together the ketchup, brown sugar, 1 teaspoon garlic powder and ½ cup chopped onions and microwave until the sugar is dissolved. Pour over meatballs and return to oven for 10 minutes.

I use a cookie scoop for an easy way to make the meatballs. I like to bake them in my mini-muffin molds. If you want more information about molds you may contact me through my website. Sheilaraellc.com.

Boiled Shrimp

4 pounds unpeeled shrimp	¼ cup kosher salt
¼ cup seafood seasoning salt	1 fresh lemon, sliced

In a 5-quart stock pot, bring 4 quarts of water to a boil. Add seasonings, lemon and shrimp. Boil 3 minutes and remove from water. Cool completely or serve hot.

The best way to tell if shrimp is done—it turns from translucent to opaque.

Breakfast Casserole

6 eggs, beaten	1 teaspoon dry mustard
1 pound sausage, cooked	2 slices bread, cubed
2 cups milk	1 cup Cheddar cheese, shredded

Beat the eggs in a 2-quart baking dish. Add the remaining ingredients and stir. Refrigerate overnight. Bake at 350 degrees for 45 minutes. Let stand for 5 minutes before inverting onto serving platter.

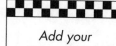

Add your favorite meat and vegetables.

I love leftover roasted vegetables in this recipe.

Breakfast in a Cup

3   cups long-grain rice, cooked
½   cup Cheddar cheese, shredded, divided
1   (4-ounce) can green chilies, chopped and drained
1   (2-ounce) jar pimientos, diced and drained

⅓   cup half-and-half
2   eggs, beaten
½   teaspoon cumin, ground
½   teaspoon salt
¼   teaspoon pepper

Preheat the oven to 400 degrees. In a large bowl mix all the ingredients except ¼ cup of cheese. Spoon into 12 muffin cups. Sprinkle with remaining cheese and bake 15 minutes or until eggs are set.

I do not mention greasing muffin tins because I use flexible molds that can withstand temperatures of 480 degrees and they do not require any preparation and clean up is swishing in hot soapy water. If you wish more information on any product used in the cookbook you may contact me through my web site. Sheilaraellc.com.

Brisket with Onion Sauce

3	pounds beef brisket	2	tablespoons olive oil
1	tablespoon red wine vinegar	1¼	cups onion, chopped
2	tablespoons salt	2	tablespoons flour
6	whole cloves	1½	cups beef broth
10	peppercorns	1	tablespoon parsley

In large saucepan, cover meat with boiling water and add vinegar, salt, cloves and peppercorn. Cover and simmer slowly for 3 hours or until meat is very tender. When done remove to platter. In the saucepan add olive oil and onions and brown for 5 minutes. Add flour and stir well; add to broth. Cook slowly stirring constantly until smooth and thickened. Add 1 tablespoon chopped parsley. Pour hot sauce over meat and serve.

Vegetables may be cooked with meat for last hour.

Cashew Pork Stir-Fry

1	tablespoon orange rind, grated	2	tablespoons vegetable oil, divided
1	tablespoon cornstarch	2	large carrots, cut diagonally
3	tablespoons soy sauce	2	celery ribs, sliced diagonally
3	tablespoons corn syrup	1	pound pork tenderloin, sliced thin
½	cup lime juice	½	cup cashews
¼	teaspoon ground ginger		

Combine orange rind, cornstarch, corn syrup, lime juice and ginger; stir well. Heat 1 tablespoon of oil in large skillet over medium heat. Add carrots and celery and stir-fry for about 3 minutes. Remove vegetables and set aside. Pour remaining oil into skillet and add pork. Stir-fry for 3 minutes. Return vegetables to pan and add soy sauce mixture and cashews. Cook, stirring constantly over medium-high heat until thickened.

This is the easiest stir-fry I have ever made and is absolutely delicious.

Chicken & Dumplings Casserole

¾ pound chicken tenders, cubed
6 baby potatoes, cubed
1 cup baby carrots, cubed
1 small red pepper, chopped
1 cup frozen green peas, thawed
2 tablespoons all-purpose flour

¼ teaspoon salt
¼ teaspoon black pepper
1 (14½-ounce) can fat-free, reduced sodium chicken broth
½ cup biscuit baking mix
¼ cup water

This is an excellent recipe with sweet potatoes and other vegetable combinations.

Preheat the oven to 400 degrees. In a 2-quart baking dish place the chicken, vegetables, flour and seasonings. Mix well. Add chicken broth and cover with waxed paper and microwave on high for 15 minutes. Combine biscuit mix and water in a bowl and mix lightly with fork. Set aside. Remove baking dish from microwave. Drop teaspoons of biscuit dough onto chicken mixture. Bake for 10 minutes or until dumplings are baked. Remove from the oven and let cool 5 minutes before serving.

I use left over vegetables from the freezer.

Chicken Casserole

1 (6-ounce) package seasoned croutons
½ cup mayonnaise
1 cup chicken broth
3 eggs, beaten
2 cups milk, divided
2½ cups chicken, cubed
½ cup green onions, chopped

1 cup carrots, chopped
½ cup celery, chopped
1 (10¾-ounce) can cream of celery soup
½ cup Swiss cheese, shredded
¼ teaspoon salt
½ teaspoon pepper to taste

Preheat the oven to 350 degrees. In a 3-quart baking dish mix croutons, mayonnaise and chicken broth together. Add eggs and 1½ cups of milk. Sauté chicken and chopped vegetables until chicken and vegetables are done. Add to baking dish. Mix ½ cup milk with soup. Pour over vegetables and top with cheese. Bake for 1 hour. Cool for 5 minutes and invert onto a serving platter.

Delicious with steamed vegetables.

This recipe comes from my great-aunt Arlyne and it is wonderful.

Chicken Crescents

2 cups diced cooked chicken
1 (3-ounce) package cream cheese
¾ cup cream of chicken soup
2 teaspoons milk

¼ teaspoon salt
⅛ teaspoon pepper
2 (8-ounce) tubes crescent rolls

Preheat the oven to 350 degrees. In a medium bowl mix the chicken, cream cheese, soup, milk, salt and pepper. Place two crescent rolls into each of the non-stick muffin cup making sure to seal seams and ends come out of cup. Spoon ½ cup of chicken mixture into each cup. Bring tops together to form a purse and seal. Bake for 25 minutes. Cool 5 minutes and unmold.

Crab and Roasted Red Pepper Strata

6	large eggs	1	teaspoon fresh rosemary, chopped
2	cups half-and-half	1	pound fresh crabmeat
3	tablespoons butter	8	cups bread cubes from crustless French bread
1	cup onions, chopped	1	teaspoon salt
½	cup celery, chopped	¾	teaspoon black pepper, ground
1	cup roasted red pepper	½	cup fresh Parmesan cheese, grated
1	garlic clove, minced		
2	tablespoons fresh chives, chopped		

Whisk eggs and half-and-half in a medium-sized bowl. Melt butter in a 3-quart baking dish. Stir in all vegetables and seasonings. Microwave on high for 3 minutes. Mix in bread crumbs. Top with crab meat and cheese. Add egg mixture. Let stand 30 minutes or cover and refrigerate overnight. Preheat the oven to 350 degrees. Bake until brown and puffed about 1 hour. Cool on rack 30 minutes. Invert onto a serving tray. Cut into wedges and serve.

I prefer fresh seafood whenever possible but frozen works fine in this recipe.

Chicken Pot Pie

1 cup red bell pepper, diced	1 tablespoon all-purpose flour
½ cup mushrooms, sliced	2 cups chicken tenders, cubed and cooked
½ cup fresh green beans, chopped	
½ cup fresh corn	½ cup fat free half-and-half
½ cup fresh peas	1 teaspoon fresh dill, minced
½ cup onion, chopped	½ teaspoon salt
½ cup celery, chopped	¼ teaspoon black pepper
½ cup fat free, reduced sodium chicken broth	2 tubes of reduced fat refrigerated crescent rolls

Preheat the oven to 375 degrees. In 2-quart baking dish place all of the vegetables with ¼ cup water and microwave for 5 minutes. Mix chicken broth and flour and pour over vegetables. Microwave for 3 minutes. Add chicken, half-and-half and seasonings. Roll out crescent rolls and place on top of chicken mixture. Bake pot pie for 15 to 20 minutes or until topping is golden and filling is bubbly.

Crockpot Stew

5 carrots, cut bite-size	½ cup tomato sauce
¼ head of cabbage	2 cups water
5 potatoes, cut bite-size	¼ cup brown sugar
1½ pounds raw stew meat	½ teaspoon salt
2 bouillon cubes	½ teaspoon pepper
1 package dry onion soup mix	

Place all ingredients into a 5-quart crockpot and cook on high for 5 to 6 hours.

This recipe is perfect for a cold winter day.

Creamy Chicken Breasts

6   whole boneless chicken breasts, skinned
½   cup all-purpose flour
1   cup butter, divided
¼   teaspoon salt
½   teaspoon pepper

1½ cups mushrooms, sliced
¾   cup wine
½   cup chicken stock
½   cup Monterey Jack cheese
½   cup Parmesan cheese

Preheat the oven to 450 degrees. Flatten chicken to about half of its original size. Coat in flour, salt and pepper. In large frying pan melt ½ cup butter and add chicken frying until golden brown. Remove the chicken and place in a 3-quart baking dish overlapping the chicken. Add wine to the pan and simmer 10 minutes. In another saucepan add ½ cup butter and sauté mushrooms for 3 minutes. Pour over chicken. When sauce has reduced pour over chicken and mushrooms. Combine the cheeses and sprinkle over chicken. Bake for 10 to 12 minutes.

Wine has a very important role in the overall taste of the dish. Use a wine that you really like. I prefer a white or a blush wine for this recipe. Never use a wine for cooking that you are just trying to get rid of.

Creamy Chicken Lasagna

5	tablespoons butter, divided	2½	cups chicken, diced and cooked
1	cup onion, chopped	3	tablespoons all-purpose flour
2	garlic cloves, minced	2	cups half-and-half
1	cup plum tomatoes, diced	½	cup dry white wine
1	cup fresh mushrooms, sliced and sautéed	3	cups shredded Monterey Jack cheese
½	teaspoon dried tarragon	1	(8-ounce) package lasagna noodles, cooked
½	teaspoon dried basil	¾	cup freshly grated Parmesan cheese
½	teaspoon sugar		
1¼	teaspoons salt, divided		

Preheat the oven to 350 degrees. Melt 2 tablespoons of the butter in a large skillet over medium heat. Add chopped onions and garlic and cook 3 to 5 minutes or until onions are transparent. Add tomatoes, mushrooms, tarragon, basil, sugar and ¼ teaspoon of the salt. Simmer 4 to 6 minutes or until sauce thickens. Stir in chicken. In a second saucepan melt remaining 3 tablespoons butter. Stir in flour and 1 teaspoon salt and cook 2 minutes. Stir in half-and-half and continue cooking for 5 to 6 minutes or until slightly thickened. Stir in wine and bring to a boil. Remove from heat. Spoon ⅓ of the tomato sauce into the bottom of pan. Cover with ⅓ of the white wine sauce. Top with 1 cup of the Monterey Jack cheese and cover with ½ of the lasagna noodles. Repeat. Top with final ⅓ of the red sauce, white sauce and remaining cheeses.

Bake 40 to 45 minutes or until heated through and light golden brown. Let stand 15 minutes and unmold.

This lasagna can be baked in the microwave for 20 minutes if time is pressing.

This recipe is a family favorite that seems to disappear as fast as I can make it.

Deli Baked Chicken Sandwich

1¼ pounds deli chicken, thin sliced
30 silver dollar buns
2   sticks butter, melted
¼   teaspoon salt

½   teaspoon fresh ground pepper
¾   ounce poppy seeds
¾   teaspoon prepared mustard

Preheat the oven to 400 degrees. In a small mixing bowl combine butter, salt, pepper, poppy seeds and mustard. Lightly spread mixture on inside of buns plus add 2 slices of chicken. Place into a 9x13-inch pan. Pour additional mixture over the top of the sandwiches. Bake for 18 to 20 minutes.

This is a great dish when you need to have things made ahead.

Dilly Salmon with a Twist

2   pounds salmon fillet
½   cup mayonnaise
¼   cup ketchup

¼   cup tomatoes, diced
4   strips bacon, cut in 1-inch pieces
1   tablespoon dill

*Fish is touchy.
DO NOT
OVERCOOK.
Fish should flake
but not be dry.
This recipe really
helps prevent
drying.*

Preheat the oven to 400 degrees. Cut salmon into six pieces. Cover the pieces with a thick layer of mayonnaise then a thin layer of ketchup and sprinkle with tomatoes, bacon and dill. Bake for 40 to 45 minutes.

Easy Chicken Divan Casserole

1 (20-ounce) package frozen cut broccoli
2 cups chicken, cooked and cubed
2 (10¾-ounce) cans cream of chicken soup, undiluted
1 cup mayonnaise
1 tablespoon fresh lemon juice
½ teaspoon curry powder
½ teaspoon chives
½ cup Cheddar cheese, shredded
½ cup soft bread crumbs
1 tablespoon butter

Preheat the oven to 350 degrees. Place broccoli in a 3-quart baking dish and microwave according to package and drain. Add chicken and set aside. Combine soup, mayonnaise, lemon juice, curry and chives in a bowl and pour over chicken and broccoli. Combine cheese, bread crumbs and butter and sprinkle over the casserole. Bake for 30 minutes.

In the summer I hate to turn on the oven so I use the microwave as much as possible. This recipe works great in the microwave.

Enchilada Casserole

1 pound lean ground beef
3 tablespoons dried onion
¾ teaspoon garlic powder
1½ teaspoons chili powder
⅛ teaspoon cumin
1 (10¾-ounce) can tomato soup
1½ cups tomato juice
6 corn tortillas, cut in 2-inch strips
1½ cups Mexican Cheddar cheese, shredded

Preheat the oven to 350 degrees. Brown ground beef and onion and drain well. Mix next 5 ingredients with ground beef. Simmer 20 minutes. Alternate layers of cheese, tortillas and meat sauce in a 3-quart baking dish. Bake uncovered 25 minutes. Sprinkle with cheese and bake 5 minutes longer or until cheese melts.

Halibut Broccoli Pie

3 cups sharp Cheddar cheese, grated, divided	1⅓ cups milk
1½ cups halibut, cooked and flaked	3 eggs, beaten
1 cup onion, finely chopped	¾ cup baking mix
1 (10-ounce) package frozen chopped broccoli, thawed and drained	½ teaspoon lemon pepper
	½ teaspoon minced garlic
	⅛ teaspoon dried thyme leaves

Preheat the oven to 400 degrees. Mix 2 cups cheese, halibut, onion and broccoli in a 2-quart baking dish. Whisk milk, eggs, baking mix, lemon pepper, garlic and thyme. Pour over halibut-broccoli mixture. Bake for 25 to 35 minutes or until a knife inserted in center comes out clean. Top with remaining cheese and bake 5 minutes longer to melt cheese. Cool 5 minutes and unmold.

Ham Loaf

1 pound ground ham	1 egg, beaten
1 pound ground pork, beef or veal	1 cup milk
2 tablespoons green peppers, chopped	1 cup bread crumbs
1 tablespoon onion, minced	½ teaspoon pepper

Salmon is also amazing in this recipe.

Preheat the oven to 350 degrees. Combine all ingredients and blend thoroughly. Press into a loaf pan. Bake 1 hour.

Butchers will grind ham for you if you ask.

This is a great brunch item because it can be made up the night before and baked in the morning.

Ham, Swiss, and Spinach Bread Pudding

1 large baguette
¼ cup butter, melted
2 onions, chopped
2 tablespoons olive oil
1 pound cooked ham, cubed
4 large eggs, beaten
4 cups whole milk

1 teaspoon salt
¼ teaspoon fresh ground nutmeg
¼ teaspoon freshly ground pepper
6 cups spinach leaves, coarsely
    chopped
¾ pound Swiss cheese, grated

Preheat the broiler. Diagonally cut baguette crosswise into ¾-inch thick slices and brush both sides with butter. Place on a non-stick lined baking sheet under the broiler and broil for 1 minute on each side. Reduce heat to 350 degrees. In a 12-inch non-stick skillet over medium-high heat add olive oil and onions stirring occasionally until golden brown. Add ham and sauté until lightly browned. In a separate bowl, whisk eggs, milk, salt, nutmeg and pepper. In a 3-quart baking dish layer bread cubes, spinach, ham mixture and cheese into 3 layers. Pour egg mixture over layers and bake 45 to 60 minutes or until puffed and edges are golden brown.

Hamburger and Olive Steak

1½ pounds ground beef
1 teaspoon salt
¼ teaspoon chili powder
¾ cup onion, minced

½ cup green olives, sliced
1 (10¾-ounce) can condensed tomato
    soup, undiluted

Preheat the oven to 400 degrees. Season the meat with salt and chili powder. Add onion and press into a 1-quart baking dish. Sprinkle sliced olives over top and pour tomato soup over the steak and bake for 30 minutes.

Hot Chicken Sandwiches

½ cup chicken broth
1 cup chicken, shredded

1 cup cracker crumbs
8 hamburger buns

In a 2-quart baking dish heat broth and chicken for 2 minutes; add crackers and heat until thick. Serve warm on buns.

This recipe is great with cheese added and then toast open faced in the oven.

Incredible Sloppy Joes

1½ pounds hamburger, browned and drained
1 (14-ounce) can sauerkraut
1½ cups ketchup
1 tablespoon prepared mustard

1 teaspoon granulated garlic
½ cup brown sugar
1 teaspoon chili powder
2 teaspoons salt
1 teaspoon seasoning salt

In a crockpot mix all ingredients and cook for 4 hours on low heat.

This is another family favorite that I serve at birthday parties because I can make it ahead.

Jalapeño-Lime Chicken

1	tablespoon olive oil		½	teaspoon fresh black pepper, ground
1	teaspoon lime zest			
2	tablespoons lime juice		¼	teaspoon salt
1	jalapeño pepper, diced		1	pound boneless, skinless chicken breast halves
1	teaspoon cumin, ground			
3	garlic cloves, crushed		6	jalapeño peppers, sliced
			½	cup black olives

Combine oil, zest, juice, jalapeño, cumin, garlic, pepper and salt in a resealable plastic bag. Place chicken in bag and press to remove air—make sure to seal tightly. Turn bag several times to coat chicken. Chill 30 minutes or up to 8 hours. Preheat grill. Place chicken on grill and cook for 6 minutes then turn and grill 8 more minutes or until internal temperature reaches 160 degrees. Garnish with jalapeño slices and black olive slices.

Jalapeño peppers can sting and irritate the skin—you should wear rubber gloves when handling peppers and do not touch eyes. Wash hands after handling.

I recommend having a meat thermometer handy anytime you grill meat. Chicken should always reach 160 degrees. If the meat is thin you can stack it and insert the thermometer through the layers for a more accurate reading.

Margie Sausage-Zucchini Impossible Pie

12 sausage links, cooked and broken
    into pieces
2 cups zucchini, shredded
1 cup tomato paste
½ cup onion, chopped
½ cup Cheddar cheese, shredded

3 eggs, beaten
1½ cups milk
¾ cup baking mix
¼ teaspoon salt
¼ teaspoon pepper

Preheat the oven to 400 degrees. In a 3-quart baking dish mix all the ingredients. Bake 30 minutes or until a knife inserted in the center comes out clean.

Meat Loaf

¾ cup dry bread crumbs
¼ cup milk
1½ pounds ground turkey
½ pound ground pork
2 eggs, beaten
½ cup onion, chopped

1 tablespoon garlic, crushed
¼ cup green pepper, chopped
1½ teaspoons salt
¾ teaspoon sage
¼ teaspoon pepper
½ cup ketchup

Preheat the oven to 350 degrees. Soak crumbs in milk and add remaining ingredients except ketchup. Mix well. Pack into a 2-quart baking dish to shape. Invert onto a non-stick lined baking sheet. Score loaf diagonally with the handle of a wooden spoon. Bake for 1 hour then fill scored marks on top with ketchup. Bake 15 minutes longer.

Mildred's Hot Dish

2   cups uncooked macaroni
4   hard-boiled eggs, diced
½   pound dried beef, chopped
½   pound American cheese, shredded

2½ cups milk
2   (10¾-ounce) cans cream of chicken
    soup

Mix all of the ingredients together the night before in the 3-quart baking dish. Preheat oven to 350 degrees. Bake for 1½ hours.

This is my grandma's recipe and I love it for it's ease of preparation.

Mom's Simply
Delicious Chicken Hot-Dish

4   cups chicken, cooked and cubed
1   (10¾-ounce) can celery soup
1   medium-large onion, sliced

1   cup American cheese, cubed
1   (2-quart) package bread dressing

Preheat the oven to 350 degrees. In a 2-quart baking dish place the chicken, soup, onion, cheese and top with dressing. Bake for 40 minutes.

This is a family recipe that has been passed on through the years from grandma, to aunts to the grandkids. I love it because it works great in the microwave.

Oven Bacon

1   pound bacon

Preheat the oven to 400 degrees. Using a baking sheet with an edge lay one layer of bacon. Bake 7 minutes and turn bacon and bake 7 more minutes.

Pepper Ricotta Primavera

1 cup ricotta cheese	1 yellow pepper, julienned
½ cup half-and-half milk	1 medium zucchini, sliced
1 garlic clove, minced	1 cup frozen peas
½ teaspoon crushed red pepper flakes	¼ teaspoon dried oregano
4 teaspoons olive or vegetable oil	¼ teaspoon dried basil
1 medium green pepper, julienned	1 (6-ounce) package fettuccine,
1 medium sweet red pepper,	cooked and drained
julienned	

In a small bowl whisk ricotta cheese and milk and set aside. In a large skillet sauté garlic and pepper flakes in oil for 1 minute. Add peppers, zucchini, peas, oregano and basil. Cook and stir over medium heat until vegetables are tender about 5 minutes then add cheese mixture and cook for additional 2 minutes. Place fettuccine in a large bowl and add vegetables and cheese mixture. Toss to coat. Serve immediately.

Pizza Hot Dish

1½ pounds hamburger	½ teaspoon sugar
¼ cup onion	½ teaspoon oregano
1 (10¾-ounce) can Cheddar cheese soup	¼ teaspoon pepper
1 (10¾-ounce) can tomato soup	4 cups frozen hash browns, thawed
¼ cup half-and-half	2 cups mozzarella cheese

Preheat the oven to 375 degrees. Brown hamburger and onion and add seasonings and pour into a 3-quart baking dish. Add the soups, half-and-half, sugar, oregano and pepper then stir well. Bake for 45 minutes. Remove and add cheese and bake an additional 15 minutes.

This is a family favorite. My mother, Marlene, always likes to try new things and this was served for Christmas Eve one year and now my family requests it often.

Pork Chop Extraordinaire

4 pork loin chops, 1-inch thick	1 tablespoon white wine
½ cup soy sauce	¼ teaspoon fresh ground pepper
4 cloves garlic, crushed	

In a large plastic zip closing bag place all ingredients and let rest in the refrigerator for 2 hours. Remove from refrigerator for 20 minutes before heating the grill. When grill is hot add chops and grill for 9 minutes. Turn and grill an additional 9 minutes. Remove from grill and cover for 5 minutes.

All good cuts of meat should be allowed to come to room temperature before cooking and allowed at least 5 minutes of resting time after the cooking process. This resting allows meat to re-absorb its juices.

Quick and Easy Crispy Fish

2   pounds red snapper
½   cup mayonnaise

3 cups Italian bread crumbs

Preheat the oven to 350 degrees. Spread snapper with mayonnaise and roll in bread crumbs. Place on a non-stick lined baking sheet and bake 20 minutes.

Pollock, salmon and sea bass all work great in place of red snapper.

Quick Mexican Lasagna

2   cups Cheddar cheese, divided
2   (10-ounce) cans chopped tomatoes and peppers
1   (16-ounce) package 10-inch tortilla shells

1   (10-ounce) can refried beans
2   cups hamburger, browned
2   cups lettuce, chopped
½   cup sour cream

Preheat the oven to 350 degrees. In a 3-quart baking dish start layering ½ cup cheese and ¼ cup tomato and peppers then top with a tortilla, refried beans and hamburger. Add another tortilla and repeat ingredients ending with a tortilla. Cover and bake for 40 minutes. Cool for 5 minutes before inverting onto a large tray. Add lettuce around the edge and sour cream on top.

Reuben Bake

1 (6-ounce) package wide noodles, cooked
4 tablespoons melted butter, divided
½ cup rye bread crumbs or rye crackers
2 cups sauerkraut

1 (12-ounce) package dried or canned corned beef
¾ cup 1000 Island dressing
2 tomatoes, sliced
1 cup Swiss cheese, shredded

Preheat the oven to 350 degrees. Toss noodles with 2 tablespoons butter. Toss the rye bread crumbs with 2 tablespoons butter. In a 2-quart baking dish layer noodles, sauerkraut, beef, dressing, tomatoes, cheese and bread. Bake for 35 minutes.

Round Steak

1 pounded round steak, cut into pieces
1 cup flour
3 tablespoons olive oil
½ cup onions, chopped

1 (10¾-once) can tomato soup
2 tablespoons Worcestershire sauce
2 tablespoons brown sugar
2 tablespoons lemon juice

Preheat the oven to 350 degrees. In a plastic bag place the flour and steak. In a large skillet heat the oil and add the steaks. Fry 4 minutes on each side. Remove and place in 2-quart baking dish. Add onions to skillet and brown then add tomato soup, Worcestershire sauce, brown sugar and lemon juice. Pour over steaks. Bake for 1½-2 hours or until tender.

Salmon Loaf

1 (16-ounce) can salmon	2 teaspoons lemon juice
¼ cup mayonnaise	1 teaspoon onion, chopped
1 egg	¼ teaspoon salt
1½ cups bread crumbs	¼ teaspoon pepper

Preheat the oven to 350 degrees. Drain salmon and remove bones. In a separate bowl mix mayonnaise, egg, bread crumbs, lemon juice, onion, salt and pepper and carefully stir in salmon. Place in buttered loaf pan and bake 45 minutes.

I prefer to use flexible molds because they reduce the clean up time and improve the overall moisture of the product.

Shrimp and Chicken Paella

¾ cup uncooked rice	1 (12-ounce) package cooked shrimp, defrosted
2 (14-ounce) cans low sodium diced tomatoes	1 (4-ounce) chicken breast, cubed
1 teaspoon saffron threads	1 cup frozen green peas, defrosted

Preheat the oven to 400 degrees. Pour rice into a 2-quart baking dish. Empty one can of tomatoes with juice over the rice, and sprinkle saffron. Add shrimp and chicken, distributing evenly. Add peas. Drain second can of tomatoes; discard juice. Distribute tomatoes over shrimp and chicken. Cover baking dish with aluminum foil. Bake for 30 minutes. Remove from oven and let rest covered for 5 minutes.

Skillet Fried Scallops

1 ¼ pounds sea scallops
¼ pound bacon, chopped

⅛ teaspoon fresh ground pepper

In a 10-inch skillet fry bacon for 3 minutes and add scallops. Sprinkle with pepper and sauté for 6 minutes.

Southwestern Chicken Shepherd's Pie

1 ½ cups salsa, medium
1 pound chicken, ground
½ teaspoon garlic, crushed
½ teaspoon fresh cilantro, chopped

4 servings instant mashed potatoes, prepared
¼ teaspoon chili powder

Preheat the oven to 400 degrees. Completely drain the salsa. Place chicken in a 2-quart baking dish and add salsa. Mix thoroughly with chicken. Add garlic, cilantro and potatoes and mix well. Spoon potatoes onto chicken and salsa making sure to cover surface completely. Score potatoes in a crosshatch pattern using tines of a fork. Spray top lightly with cooking spray. Bake for 30 minutes. Remove from oven and let rest for 5 minutes. Before serving sprinkle casserole with chili powder.

Sweet and Sour Chicken Breasts

2	pounds boneless chicken breasts		2	tablespoons lemon juice
2	tablespoons oil		4	tablespoons oil, divided
3	tablespoons ketchup		½	teaspoon onion powder
3	tablespoons sugar		¼	teaspoon pepper
2	tablespoons soy sauce			

Preheat the oven to 350 degrees. In a 10-inch skillet heat oil and add chicken and sauté 5 minutes. In microwave-proof measuring cup add remaining ingredients and heat 3 minutes or until mixture comes to a boil. Pour over chicken and bake 15 minutes.

Swordfish Fettuccine with Sugar Snap Peas

1	(12-ounce) package sugar snap peas, trimmed		1	tablespoon all-purpose flour
2	cups carrots, julienned		½	cup clam juice
1	(8-ounce) package fettuccine, cooked		½	cup canned low salt chicken broth
2	teaspoons olive oil		½	cup dry white wine
1	pound skinless swordfish steaks, cubed		1½	tablespoons fresh lemon juice
3	tablespoons fresh parsley, chopped		½	teaspoon chili powder
4	green onions, thinly sliced		¼	teaspoon pepper
			¼	teaspoon salt
				Lemon wedges

Blanch peas in medium saucepan of boiling salted water 1 minute. Add carrots and blanch 1 minute longer. Drain. Rinse under cold water and drain well. Heat oil in a large non-stick skillet over high heat. Sprinkle fish with salt and pepper. Add fish to skillet and sauté until golden brown and almost cooked through about 2 minutes. Using slotted spoon transfer fish to plate. Cover to keep warm. Add parsley, onions and flour to skillet and cook for 30 seconds. Add clam juice, broth, wine and lemon juice. Simmer until sauce thickens stirring constantly about 2 minutes. Add sugar snap peas, carrots, pasta, chili powder, pepper and salt and continue cooking for 1 minute. Add fish cook until heated through about 1 minute.

Taco Pie

1	pound ground turkey	2	cups Cheddar cheese, shredded
1	package taco seasoning	2	cups lettuce, shredded
1	teaspoon pepper	1	cup tomato, diced
1	tablespoon fresh garlic, chopped	½	cup sour cream
¼	cup chopped onion	1	cup salsa
1	(8-ounce) tube crescent rolls		

Preheat the oven to 350 degrees. In a 10-inch skillet brown turkey, taco seasoning, pepper, garlic and onion and then drain. Line a 2-quart baking dish with crescent rolls. Bake until crust is lightly brown. Top with ground turkey mixture and spread with cheese. Bake 20 minutes or until cheese melts. Serve with lettuce, tomatoes, sour cream and salsa.

Tamale Pie

4	teaspoons olive oil, divided	1	fresh green chili, chopped
1	cup onions, chopped	2	cups canned crushed tomatoes
3	tablespoons garlic, crushed	½	cup Cheddar cheese, shredded
1	tablespoon cumin	¾	cup cornmeal
1	teaspoon coriander	1	tablespoon white flour
1	teaspoon oregano	½	teaspoon salt
1	teaspoon pepper	1	teaspoon baking powder
1	cup carrots, diced	¼	teaspoon baking soda
1	cup red peppers, diced	2	egg whites
1	cup zucchini, diced	½	cup buttermilk

Preheat the oven to 400 degrees. Sauté together 2 teaspoons olive oil, onions, garlic, cumin, coriander, oregano, pepper, carrots, peppers, zucchini, chili and tomatoes. Mix well and pour into a 2-quart baking dish. Top with the cheese. In a separate mixing bowl combine cornmeal, flour, salt, baking powder and baking soda. In a separate bowl combine egg whites, buttermilk and olive oil. Gently fold wet ingredients into the dry ingredients. Pour over vegetable mixture and bake for 30 to 35 minutes.

Tater-Tot Casserole

1	(10¾-ounce) can celery cream soup	½	teaspoon seasoning salt
1	cup sour cream	½	teaspoon pepper
½	cup milk	1½	cups sharp Cheddar cheese, divided
1	(16-ounce) package tater-tots, thawed	1½	pounds hamburger, browned

Preheat the oven to 350 degrees. Mix soup, sour cream, milk, salt, pepper, and ½ cup cheese. Place hamburger in a 3-quart baking dish and layer with soup mixture then the tater-tots. Bake for 30 minutes. Spread with remaining cheese. Bake another 20 minutes.

This recipe comes from another dear friend who I call my Michigan mom and grandma. Carolyn came into our lives purely by the grace of God and has remained a very important part of my family life.

Tuna Pies

1	(12-ounce) package quick frozen mixed vegetables, cooked	1½	cups sifted all-purpose flour
1	(7-ounce) can tuna, drained and flaked	1½	teaspoons salt
		¼	cup creamy peanut butter
1	(10¾-ounce) can cream of onion soup	½	cup shortening
		2-3	tablespoons cold water

Preheat the oven to 375 degrees. Combine vegetables, tuna and soup. Mix well and set aside while you make the pastry. Combine flour and salt. Add peanut butter and shortening and cut in with a pastry blender. Sprinkle mixture with cold water and blend in lightly (the pastry should hold together and form ball). Roll out ½ of pastry onto non-stick surface. Line a 1-quart baking dish with pastry. Fill with tuna and vegetable mixture. Roll remaining pastry to fit casserole for top crust and crimped edge. Make holes in the center. Bake for 20 to 25 minutes.

Turkey Broccoli Wrap

2 tablespoons vegetable oil
⅛ teaspoon garlic, crushed
¾ cup fresh mushrooms, sliced
¼ teaspoon salt
¼ teaspoon pepper
¾ cup broccoli florets
⅛ cup carrots, grated

¼ cup water chestnuts, sliced
2 tablespoons chicken or turkey broth
¾ teaspoon soy sauce
¼ teaspoon ground ginger
1½ cups cooked turkey, diced
6 flour tortillas

Heat oil in a large skillet and add garlic. Cook 30 seconds and add mushrooms sprinkled with salt and pepper. Add broccoli, carrots, water chestnuts, turkey broth, soy sauce and ginger. Cook 4 to 5 minutes until broccoli is tender and liquid is evaporated then add hot turkey and stir. Warm tortillas according to package instructions and fill with turkey.

Turkey Casserole

1 cup chicken soup
½ cup mayonnaise
1½ teaspoons lime juice
½ teaspoon mustard
⅛ teaspoon curry powder
1 (10-ounce) package frozen
   vegetables

1 cup water chestnuts
1 (4-ounce) can bamboo shoots
2 cups turkey, cooked
⅔ cup Cheddar cheese, shredded
¼ cup seasoned bread crumbs

Preheat the oven to 350 degrees. Combine soup, mayonnaise, lime juice, mustard and curry powder for the sauce and mix well. Drain and defrost vegetables. In a 2-quart baking dish layer half of each item, starting with vegetable, turkey, sauce, water chestnuts, bamboo shoots, and cheese. Repeat. Top with bread crumbs and bake for 45 minutes.

SIMPLE SIDES

Side Dishes

Amazing Fruit Salad

1   (3.9-ounce) package instant vanilla
      pudding mix
2   tablespoons instant orange juice mix
1   (20-ounce) can pineapple

2   kiwi, chunked
2   bananas, chunked
4   cups fresh strawberries, chunked
1   apple, chunked

Drain pineapple juice and mix it with the dry pudding mix and orange mix. Pour over fruit and stir.

This recipe came from my mentor teacher as I was completing my student teaching in Madison, South Dakota. Mrs. Keiner and her husband Bill had me over for supper and I fell in love with this wonder salad.

Baked Corn and Tomatoes

2   cups fresh kernel corn
2   cups Roma tomatoes, chopped
1   teaspoon salt
1   teaspoon sugar

⅛   teaspoon pepper
1   cup fresh bread crumbs
3   tablespoons bacon drippings

Preheat the oven to 375 degrees. Mix corn and tomatoes with seasonings. Pour into a 2-quart baking dish. Mix bread crumbs and bacon drippings and spread evenly over corn and tomatoes. Bake for 30 minutes.

Bread Stuffing

4	cups dry bread, cubed	½	teaspoon poultry seasoning
3	tablespoons onion, chopped	¼	teaspoon fresh sage
1	teaspoon salt	⅓	cup butter, melted
¼	teaspoon pepper	1	(15-ounce) can chicken broth

Preheat the oven to 350 degrees. In a 3-quart baking dish mix all ingredients. Toss and bake for 20 minutes.

Broccoli Ring

2	pounds broccoli	2	cups cream onion soup
½	cup Cheddar blend cheese, shredded	1	teaspoon salt
3	eggs, separated	½	teaspoon pepper

Preheat the oven to 325 degrees. Chop broccoli into bite-size pieces and place into a 1½-quart mold with ¼ cup water. Cover and microwave for 3 minutes or until tender. Mix cheese, soup and beaten egg yolks. Whip egg whites and fold into mixture. Pour over broccoli and lightly toss to coat broccoli. Bake for about 40 minutes in a water bath. Remove from oven and let rest 5 minutes. Invert onto a serving platter.

Water baths are done to create an even bake from the edge of the product to the center. I recommend it for cheese cakes or other egg based products that have a tendency of drying out.

Calico Beans

1	(15-ounce) can red beans, drained	1	tablespoon vinegar
1	(15-ounce) can pork and beans	1	small onion, chopped
1	(15-ounce) can butter beans	½	pound sausage, cooked
½	cup brown sugar	½	pound bacon, cooked
½	cup ketchup		

Preheat the oven to 350 degrees. Mix all the ingredients in a 3-quart baking dish and bake 45 minutes.

Cauliflower Patties

1	small head cauliflower, cut into florets	1	tablespoon fresh chives
1	teaspoon coriander seed	1	teaspoon sea salt
2	eggs	⅛	teaspoon fresh ground pepper
2	tablespoons flour	⅛	teaspoon nutmeg
1	tablespoon fresh parsley	2	tablespoons olive oil

Boil cauliflower and coriander in a 5-quart stock pot for 9-11 minutes and drain and allow cooling. Preheat the oven to 400 degrees. Mash florets and add the eggs, flour, parsley, chives, salt, pepper, nutmeg and oil. Using a cookie scoop, scoop 20 patties onto a non-stick lined baking. Bake 20 minutes or until golden brown.

This is a great low-carb recipe.

Cauliflower Salad

1	head cauliflower, cubed	1	cup mayonnaise
1	(16-ounce) package frozen peas	3	tablespoons milk
1	celery stack, chopped	1	tablespoon dry Italian salad
1	green onion, chopped		dressing mix

Mix all the ingredients. Refrigerate 2 hours.

This recipe is similar to one that was share with me by one of my students at Reading High School. I really did not care for cauliflower until he brought it to one of our Mock Weddings.

Cheesy Eggs

2	tablespoons butter	1	teaspoon mustard
¼	cup American cheese, cubed	⅛	teaspoon cayenne pepper
⅓	cup half-and-half	6	eggs, beaten

Preheat the oven to 375 degrees. In a 2-quart baking dish combine all ingredients. Bake for 30 or until set.

Cheesy Broccoli Pockets

1   pound fresh chopped broccoli, steamed
1   clove garlic, minced
1   cup mozzarella cheese, shredded
⅓   cup Parmesan cheese, grated
¼   cup roasted red peppers, coarsely chopped

1   tablespoon fresh oregano, chopped
½   teaspoon salt
¼   teaspoon black pepper
1   batch Simply Sheila Rae bread dough recipe

Preheat the oven to 375 degrees. In a medium skillet heat oil over low heat and add the garlic. Sauté for 2 minutes. Add broccoli and stir until moisture has evaporated, about 3 minutes. Remove from heat and cool slightly. In a medium bowl combine broccoli mixture, mozzarella, Parmesan, roasted peppers, oregano, salt and pepper and mix well. On a lightly floured surface, divide dough into 8 pieces and roll out each piece to form a 6-inch circle. Spoon an equal amount of broccoli mixture in the center of each circle. Fold dough over filling to form a half circle. Press edges with a fork to seal. Prick holes into pocket tops. Place pockets onto a non-stick lined baking sheet. Bake 25 minutes or until golden.

Christmas Ribbon Salad

2   (16-ounce) cans pitted sour cherries
2   (3-ounce) packages cherry flavored gelatin
1   envelope unflavored gelatin
2   cups boiling water
⅓   cup sugar
½   cup Port or sweet red wine
¼   cup lemon juice
1   (8-ounce) package cream cheese, softened
½   cup walnuts, toasted and chopped

Drain cherries and reserve 1 cup juice. Chop cherries. Stir together gelatins and boiling water until dissolved. Stir in the reserved juice, sugar, wine and lemon juice. Stir in cherries. Pour half of gelatin mixture into a 2-quart decorative mold. Let set 2 hours or until almost set. Stir together remaining gelatin mixture, cream cheese and walnuts; make sure to blend well. Pour over slightly set gelatin mixture in mold. Chill 6 hours or until firm. Unmold onto a serving tray.

Garnish with whipped cream and fresh cranberries.

Run your finger around the top of the gelatin to release from the mold before inverting on serving tray.

Cottage Cheese Salad

1   (16-ounce) carton cottage cheese
1   (3-ounce) package orange gelatin
1   (11-ounce) can Mandarin oranges, drained
1   (8-ounce) carton non-dairy whipping cream

Mix the cottage cheese, gelatin and oranges together. Fold in whipped topping. Chill.

This is a perfect item for a potluck when time is of an essence.

Creamy Potato Casserole

½ cup butter	1 cup Monterey Jack cheese, shredded
½ cup onion, chopped	1 green pepper, diced
1 (16-ounce) package frozen hash browns	¼ teaspoon pepper
1 (10¾-ounce) can cream of chicken soup	1 cup cheese crackers, crushed, divided
1 (10¾-ounce) can milk	

Preheat the oven to 375 degrees. In a shallow 2-quart baking dish place onions and butter and microwave for 5 minutes. Add potatoes, soup, milk, cheese, peppers and ½ cup crackers. Stir and top with remaining crackers. Bake for 40 minutes.

Fancy Sweet Potatoes

½ cup brown sugar	⅛ teaspoon cinnamon
2 tablespoons cornstarch	5 sweet potatoes, cooked, cubed
¼ teaspoon salt	½ cup pecan, chopped
1 cup orange juice	1 cup mini marshmallows
2 tablespoons butter	

Preheat the oven to 350 degrees. In a 3-quart baking dish combine sugar, cornstarch, salt, orange juice, butter and cinnamon. Boil in the microwave for 2 minutes. Add sweet potatoes and stir. Bake for 25 minutes. Top with marshmallows and pecans. Return to oven for 5 minutes.

Garden Fresh Salad

4	cucumbers, sliced	1	tablespoon salt
1	carrot, thinly sliced	1	tablespoon celery seed
1	green pepper, chopped	2	cups sugar
2	medium onions, chopped	1	cup vinegar

Mix the vegetables in one bowl. Dissolve sugar in vinegar and add remaining seasonings. Pour on vegetables and toss. Refrigerate overnight.

Grace's Stuffed Peppers

1	pound spicy sausage	2	teaspoons Worcestershire sauce
2	tablespoons onions, chopped	2	slices soft bread soaked in ¼ cup milk
1	tablespoon celery, chopped		
1	teaspoon salt	1	egg
¼	teaspoon poultry seasoning	6	medium green peppers, cleaned and seeded
⅛	teaspoon pepper		
⅛	teaspoon dry mustard	½	cup tomato juice

Preheat the oven to 350 degrees. Mix all ingredients but the peppers and tomato juice in a mixing bowl. Fill well of each pepper full. Stand peppers on end in a non-stick baking dish. Pour tomato juice in pan and bake covered for 1 hour.

Gram Grayces' Baked Beans

1 (32-ounce) can great Northern beans	2 tablespoons tomato purée or sauce
½ cup onion, chopped	¼ cup dark brown sugar
2 tablespoons butter	1 tablespoon powdered mustard
2 tablespoons garlic, crushed	½ pound bacon, cooked and crumbed

Preheat the oven to 350 degrees. In a 3-quart baking dish place chopped onion, butter and garlic and microwave for 5 minutes. Stir in remaining ingredients. Cover and bake for 30 to 45 minutes.

This is my husband's grandma's recipe and loved by all.

Lemon Salad

2 (3.9-ounce) cooked lemon pie filling mix	1 (15-ounce) can fruit cocktail, drained
¼ cup lemon juice	1 (20-ounce) can crushed pineapple
1 cup cream, whipped	2 cups miniature marshmallows

Mix the pie filling, juice, fruit and marshmallows. Fold in whipping cream and chill overnight.

Make for Later Mashed Potatoes

9 pounds of potatoes, cooked
1 (6-ounce) package cream cheese
½ cup American cheese, shredded
1 cup plain yogurt

1 teaspoon onion salt
1 teaspoon garlic salt
½ teaspoon pepper
2 tablespoons butter

In a large mixing bowl place all ingredients and mix until smooth. Place in a 3-quart baking dish. Cover and refrigerate until needed. Preheat oven to 350 degrees and bake for 50 minutes.

These potatoes can be made 2 days ahead and reheated.

Mashed Potatoes

6 potatoes, medium sized, cubed
3 tablespoons butter

3 teaspoons salt, divided
⅓ cup hot milk or cream

Place potatoes into a large saucepan and add enough water to cover potatoes plus 2 teaspoons salt. Boil for 20 minutes or until fork tender. Drain. Place potatoes into mixing bowl. Whip potatoes with the remaining ingredients until smooth.

Add a teaspoon prepared horseradish. Replace cream or milk with flavored sour cream or cream cheese. Add your favorite cheese. Add seasonings such as dill or rosemary.

Pearl Onion Gratin

1	(16-ounce) bag frozen small whole onions	⅓	cup grated Romano cheese
1	(16-ounce) jar white sauce	¼	teaspoon dried thyme
2	tablespoons butter	⅛	teaspoon red pepper, crushed
½	cup plain, dried bread crumbs	⅛	teaspoon nutmeg, ground
		½	teaspoon fresh parsley, chopped

Preheat the oven to 325 degrees. In a 2-quart baking dish prepare onions according to microwave directions. Drain onions in colander and set aside. Stir in white sauce. Meanwhile, in a small microwave-safe bowl melt butter in the microwave oven on high for 30 to 45 seconds. Stir in bread crumbs, Romano, thyme, crushed red pepper and nutmeg. Spoon the bread-crumb mixture evenly over onion mixture. Bake uncovered for 35 to 40 minutes or until the edges bubble and top browns slightly. Garnish with parsley.

Peppy Potatoes

¼	cup olive oil	¼	teaspoon fresh ground pepper
4	tablespoons seasoned coating mix for chicken	8	medium potatoes, wedged

Preheat the oven to 350 degrees. Mix oil, pepper and seasoning mix. Toss potatoes wedges. Lay on a non-stick lined baking sheet. Bake for 45 to 50 minutes or until tender.

Puffed Potatoes

3	cups potatoes, mashed		½	teaspoon salt
1	cup cream		½	teaspoon pepper
2	egg yolks		½	cup Monterey Jack cheese, shredded
3	egg whites			
3	tablespoons butter			

Preheat the oven to 375 degrees. Beat mashed potatoes, cream, egg yolks, butter, salt and pepper. Fold in stiffly beaten egg whites. Place into a non-stick baking dish and top with butter and cheese. Bake until puffed and golden brown.

Roasted Sweet Potato Salad

2½	pounds sweet potatoes, cubed		1	cup non-fat yogurt
2	tablespoons olive oil		1	tablespoon fresh cilantro, minced
1	green pepper, chopped		1	teaspoon chives
3	stalks celery, chopped		2	teaspoons lime juice
¼	cup onion, chopped		⅛	teaspoon salt
1	fresh chili, chopped			

Preheat the oven 400 degrees. On a non-stick baking sheet, toss sweet potatoes and olive oil. Bake 15 minutes or until tender. Cool. In a 3-quart baking dish mix remaining ingredients. Stir in sweet potatoes. Refrigerate overnight.

Scalloped Pineapple

4	cups stale bread, cubed		1	(20-ounce) can crushed pineapple, drained
1	cup butter		3	eggs, beaten
1	cup granulated sugar		1/8	teaspoon cinnamon

Preheat the oven to 350 degrees. In a 2-quart baking dish melt butter and add sugar, pineapple and eggs making sure to mix well. Sprinkle with cinnamon and 1 teaspoon sugar. Bake uncovered for 40 to 45 minutes.

This is one of my great-aunts recipes and is absolutely delicious. I like to serve it with ice cream.

Spicy Black Bean and Rice Frittata

1	(15-ounce) can black bean		1	medium zucchini, coarsely chopped
1	medium onion, chopped		1	egg yolk, beaten
3	garlic cloves, minced		1	egg, beaten
1	red bell pepper, diced		1/4	cup fresh coriander leaves, chopped
1/2	teaspoon dried hot red pepper flakes		1 1/2	teaspoons salt
3	tablespoons butter		1/4	teaspoon freshly ground black pepper
1/3	cup long-grained white rice		1/8	teaspoon hot sauce
2/3	cup water			

Preheat the oven 350 degrees. In a 3-quart baking dish cook onion, garlic, bell pepper, red pepper flakes and butter in the microwave for 3 minutes. Add rice and water then cover with plastic wrap and cook until rice is tender and water is absorbed, about 8 minutes. Add remaining ingredients. Stir well and bake for 20 minutes or until frittata is golden and set. Unmold onto a serving tray.

Garnish with guacamole and sour cream.

SIMPLY BREAD

Breads

48 Tortillas

6	cups flour	1	cup shortening or lard
2	teaspoons baking powder	2	cups water
2	teaspoons salt		

My preference is lard; the fat content makes a lighter tortilla.

Mix flour, baking powder and salt in a bowl. Using a pastry cutter cut in shortening. Slowly add water. Work into a large ball. Cut into 48 balls; roll thin on a non-stick surface. Heat 10-inch skillet over medium heat and cook tortillas on both sides until lightly browned.

Tortillas are fabulous with cheese, or just butter and sugar.

Blueberry Scones

2	cups all-purpose flour	1	egg
¼	cup granulated sugar	½	cup buttermilk
2	teaspoons baking powder	1¼	cups fresh blueberries
½	teaspoon salt	1	cup powdered sugar
⅓	cup butter	2	tablespoons lemon juice

Preheat the oven to 400 degrees. In a large mixing bowl, combine flour, granulated sugar, baking powder and salt. Cut in butter until mixture resembles coarse crumbs. Beat together egg and buttermilk. Add egg mixture and blueberries to flour mixture; stir with fork only until combined. Bring together into a ball; pat or lightly roll dough to ½-inch thickness. Cut dough into 8 equal pieces. Place on a non-stick lined cooking sheet. Bake for 11 to 13 minutes or until light golden brown. In a small bowl, combine powdered sugar and juice; mix well. Drizzle glaze over hot scones. Serve warm.

Buttermilk is a wonderful product, but I don't always have it on hand so I add 1 tablespoon vinegar to every ½ cup of milk.

Frozen blueberries work, but don't thaw.

Breakfast Bread

2¾ cups bread flour
2¾ cups whole wheat flour
1¾ teaspoons baking soda
½ teaspoon salt
3 tablespoons butter, softened

2¾ cups buttermilk
1 egg
1 teaspoon water
2 teaspoons oatmeal, finely ground

Preheat the oven to 350 degrees. Whisk bread flour, whole wheat flour, baking soda and salt together in a large mixing bowl. Using a pastry blender, cut butter into flour mixture until it resembles coarse meal. Gradually add buttermilk, stirring with a wooden spoon until dough comes together. Turn dough out onto a non-stick surface. Dust hands with flour and knead with the heels of your hands until dough is semi-smooth, about 1 minute. Divide dough in half. Shape each piece of dough into a 6-inch round. Cut each dough round into 3 equal triangles and arrange on a large non-stick baking sheet 3 to 4 inches apart. Beat egg and water together in a small bowl. Using pastry brush, brush tops of triangles with egg wash and sprinkle each with a little oatmeal. Bake loaves until deep golden brown and hollow sounding when tapped, about 60 minutes. Set aside to cool on a wire rack for at least 15 minutes before serving.

Serve with fresh jelly or jam.

Buttermilk can be substituted with sour milk: 1 tablespoon vinegar to every ½ cup of milk. Let stand 3 minutes.

Cheddar Cheese Scones

2¼ cups self-rising flour
1 tablespoon granulated sugar
2 teaspoons baking powder
¼ cup fresh chives, minced
1¼ cups extra sharp Cheddar cheese,
    shredded

¾ cup whole milk
2 large eggs, divided
1 tablespoon vegetable oil
2 teaspoons spicy mustard
⅛ cup sesame seeds

Preheat the oven to 425 degrees. Whisk first 3 ingredients in large bowl. Stir in chives and cheese. Whisk milk, 1 egg, oil, and mustard in small bowl. Gradually add milk mixture to dry ingredients, tossing until moist clumps form and add more milk by tablespoonfuls if dough is dry. Turn dough onto lightly floured surface. Knead just until dough comes together. Pat out dough into 1-inch thick round. Using 2½-inch diameter cutter cut scones. Gather dough scraps and repeat. Transfer to a non-stick lined baking sheet. Whisk remaining egg in small cup; brush over scones. Sprinkle with sesame seeds. Bake 14 to 15 minutes or until golden on top and tester comes out clean. Cool scones on sheet 5 minutes. Transfer to basket. Serve warm.

Cheese Garlic Biscuits

4 cups all-purpose baking mix
1⅓ cups sour milk
½ cup Monterey Jack cheese,
    shredded

½ cup butter or margarine, melted
1 tablespoon fresh parsley, minced
1 teaspoon garlic powder

Stir together baking mix, milk, and cheese until soft dough forms. Drop by heaping tablespoonfuls onto a non-stick lined baking sheet. Bake at 450 degrees for 6 to 8 minutes or until golden. Stir together butter, parsley and garlic powder; brush over warm biscuits.

Sour milk is made by adding vinegar to milk: 1 tablespoon of vinegar to every ½ cup of milk. Check out my website for more ideas, sheilaraellc.com.

Chocolate Chip Cherry Cream Muffins

2   cups frozen or canned unsweetened
    tart cherries, divided
½   cup butter
1¼ cups granulated sugar, divided
2   eggs
1   teaspoon almond extract

1   teaspoon vanilla extract
2   cups all-purpose flour
2   teaspoons baking powder
½   teaspoon salt
½   cup light cream
½   cup chocolate chips

Preheat the oven to 375 degrees. Cut cherries in halves while frozen. Set aside to thaw and drain well. In a large mixing bowl, beat butter and 1 cup sugar until light and fluffy. Add eggs, almond and vanilla extract, beating well. Crush ½ cup cherries with a fork; add to batter.

Sift flour, baking powder and salt. Fold in ½ the flour mixture with a spatula, then ½ the cream. Add remaining flour and cream. Fold in remaining cherry halves and chocolate chips. Portion batter evenly into a 12 cup muffin tray and sprinkle with ¼ cup sugar. Bake for 20 to 30 minutes or until golden brown. Cool 5 minutes and remove.

Muffin recipes can always be baked in loaf pans if you prefer. I love to try out new shapes of muffin molds. It makes life more interesting.

Chocolate Chunk Muffins

2½ cups semi-sweet chocolate chunks, divided
6 tablespoons unsweetened cocoa powder
2 teaspoons vanilla
⅔ cup whole milk

1 cup all-purpose flour
½ teaspoon baking soda
½ teaspoon salt
½ cup butter, softened
1 cup granulated sugar
2 large eggs

Preheat the oven to 350 degrees. Melt ½ cup semi-sweet chunks in the microwave on 20% power and add cocoa powder. Cool slightly. Add vanilla and milk. Whisk together flour, baking soda, and salt. Beat butter add sugar in a large bowl with an electric mixer until pale and fluffy. Add eggs one at a time beating well after each addition. Add chocolate mixture and beat well. Mix in flour and chocolate mixture alternately, scraping the side of bowl after each addition. Fold in remaining chunks. Portion batter evenly into a 12-cup muffin tray and bake 18 to 22 minutes. Cool 5 minutes and invert onto a cooling rack.

I prefer the silicone and glass muffin molds for this recipe.

Classic Banana Muffins

2	cups all-purpose flour		2	large eggs
¾	teaspoon baking soda		1½	cups mashed ripe banana
½	teaspoon salt		⅓	cup sour cream
1	cup brown sugar		2	teaspoons vanilla extract
¼	cup butter, softened			

Preheat the oven to 350 degrees. Lightly spoon flour into dry measuring cup; level with a spatula. Combine the flour, baking soda and salt, stirring with a whisk. Place sugar and butter in a large bowl and beat with a mixer at medium speed for 1 minute. Add the eggs, banana, sour cream and vanilla; beat until blended. Add flour mixture; beat at low speed just until moist. Portion batter evenly into a 12-cup muffin tray and bake for 20 to 30 minutes or until a wooden pick inserted in center comes out clean.

Coconut Bread

4	eggs, beaten		1	cup buttermilk
3	cups granulated sugar, divided		2	cups coconut
1	cup oil		1	cup walnuts
½	teaspoon salt		½	cup water
3	cups flour		2	tablespoons butter
½	teaspoon baking powder		2	teaspoons coconut flavoring
½	teaspoon baking soda			

Preheat the oven to 325 degrees. Beat eggs and 2 cups sugar until light creamy color. Add oil. Sift together all dry ingredients. Add buttermilk and dry ingredients by alternating. Stir in coconut and nuts and bake 60 minutes in 2 large loaf molds. When done boil 1 cup sugar, water and butter for 5 minutes. Add coconut flavoring. Pour over breads while still in pan. Cool completely before removing from pan.

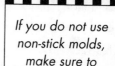

If you do not use non-stick molds, make sure to spray them well.

I use flexible molds for all my baking to ensure a highly moist product.

This recipe is another that came from a dear friend Linda Sheriff in North Carolina back when I was teaching Commercial Foods to high school students.

Cream Puffs

1	cup water	½	teaspoon salt
½	cup butter	4	eggs
1	cup flour		

Preheat the oven to 400 degrees. Heat the water and butter in a medium saucepan. Bring to a boil and add flour and salt stirring batter over heat until it leaves the sides of the pan and forms a ball. Remove from heat and cool slightly. Add one egg at a time, beating well after each addition. Place spoonfuls of batter 2-inches apart on a non-stick lined baking sheet, heaping them well in the center. Bake for 25 to 30 minutes. Test by tapping on puffs. They should sound hollow. Cool completely.

My favorite way of serving them is filled with chicken salad or fresh whipped cream.

Grandma Landsman's Dark Buns

1½	cups scalded milk	½	cup warm water
½	cup granulated sugar	1	egg
⅓	cup vegetable oil	2	cups whole wheat flour
2	teaspoons salt	3½-4	cups white flour
2	tablespoons yeast		

Heat milk in microwave for 2 minutes; add sugar, oil and salt. Let cool. Dissolve yeast in water. Add to mixture. Add egg and beat well. Add flour slowly until soft dough forms. Knead for 10 minutes. Let rise. Punch down once and then shape into buns. Bake at 350 degrees for 30 to 35 minutes.

This recipe comes from my Grandma Landsman. It was made for every family get together that I can remember. It was a battle among the grandkids to get the ends because they were the best. My grandma made these wonderful rolls for a local hospital as their baker for years and we were just fortunate to get them on special days. Grandma shared how to make these with me years ago, but they will never be the same as Grandma's.

Homemade Noodles

1¼ cups flour
1   egg, beaten
½   teaspoon salt

2   teaspoons oil
2   tablespoons milk

Mound flour onto a non-stick surface, make a well in center. Combine egg, salt, oil and milk; place in well. Slowly work flour into egg mixture. Work dough until stiff. Cover and let rest 20 minutes. Roll on a non-stick surface to desired thickness. Roll dough up like a jelly roll and slice ⅛-inch thick. Spread out strips and dry 2 hours. Drop into boiling soup or stock and cook for 5 to 10 minutes.

There is only one way to really tell if noodles are done, taste.

Honeyed Apple Scones

2   cups flour
⅔   cup + 2 teaspoons wheat germ, divided
2   teaspoons baking powder
1¼ teaspoons cinnamon, divided
¼   teaspoon baking soda
¼   teaspoon salt

¼   teaspoon ground nutmeg
⅓   cup cold butter
1   large tart apple, chopped
½   cup milk
¼   cup honey
2   teaspoons granulated sugar

Preheat the oven to 400 degrees. In a large bowl combine flour, ⅔ cup wheat germ, baking powder, 1 teaspoon cinnamon, baking soda, salt and nutmeg. Using a pasty blender cut in the butter until the mixture resembles coarse crumbs. Combine the apple, milk and honey; add to dry ingredients just until moistened. Turn onto a floured surface and knead gently 5 to 6 times. Gently pat dough into a 9-inch circle that is ½-inch thick. Combine 2 teaspoons wheat germ, sugar and ¼ teaspoon cinnamon; sprinkle over dough. Cut into eight wedges and place on a non-stick lined baking sheet. Bake for 15 to 18 minutes.

Instantly Delicious Cinnamon Rolls

12 frozen cinnamon rolls
1   (3.9-ounce) package instant vanilla
    pudding
1   cup ice cream

½   cup butter
1   tablespoon vanilla
1   teaspoon salt

Place frozen cinnamon rolls in 9x13x2-inch pan before going to bed. Melt ice cream and butter; add vanilla and salt. Pour over rolls. Cover and let rest on counter overnight. In the morning preheat the oven to 350 degrees and bake rolls 20 to 25 minutes. Cool 5 minutes and invert onto a non-stick lined baking sheet.

I use a 3-quart non-stick mold to make these rolls because it eliminates the clean-up.

Johnny Cake Cornbread

2   cups self-rising cornmeal
3   tablespoons sugar
2   cups buttermilk

1   large egg, beaten
⅓   cup butter, melted

Preheat the oven to 400 degrees. Combine dry ingredients in one bowl and wet ingredients in a second. Combine but do not over mix. Pour into a 2-quart baking dish. Bake for 25 minutes or until golden brown. Invert onto serving platter.

We enjoyed this throughout the winter for supper. My father, Bill, enjoyed his with warm milk and sugar. My sister and I thought that a little odd; but he loved it.

Jorenby Lefsa

3	cups rice or mashed potatoes	1	teaspoon salt
¼	cup granulated sugar	1-1½	cups flour
¼	cup half-and-half		

Mix together potatoes, sugar, half-and-half, and salt. Refrigerate for 20 minutes before adding the flour. Make into small balls and roll out almost paper thin and bake on a hot lefsa griddle until golden brown and small bubbles form.

To rice potatoes you need a ricer—it looks like a large garlic press. If you don't have a lefsa griddle you can use a large flat frying pan.

Grandma Jorenby was famous for her amazing lefsa and little did she know that lefsa would make a big splash in American culture. We are looking for alternatives to high fat and high carbohydrate foods and just the other day I saw lefsa as an alternative bread source.

What I remember about this wonderful bread was that my Grandpa Jorenby would sit next to me at family meal and prepare it just right. I was always so full leaving the table that I would feel sick. Grandpa and Grandma loved to please their family and friends with great food.

Long Johns Fried Doughnuts

½	cup vegetable shortening	2	eggs, beaten
1	cup boiling water	½	teaspoon nutmeg
1	cup evaporated milk	½	cup sugar
½	teaspoon vanilla	2	teaspoons salt
2¾	tablespoons yeast	8½-9	cups flour
½	warm water		

Combine the shortening, boiling water, milk and vanilla. Dissolve yeast in warm water. Stir yeast mixture into shortening mixture. Be sure shortening mixture is lukewarm. Add remaining ingredients. Knead well for 5 minutes. Let rest for 10 minutes. Roll out ¼-inch thick and cut into 1x6-inch pieces. Let rise for 1 hour. Heat the oil in a fryer to 375 degrees. Slowly lower raised side into hot oil and fry 2 minutes and turn and fry 2 additional minutes.

Doughnuts should be lightly browned on both sides. I always practice on one, because of thickness and size of doughnut, to make sure they are done all the way through.

I fill and frost these with the Best Frosting Ever recipe found in the Candy and Frosting section.

Mom's Bran Muffins

3 cups 100% bran	2 eggs, beaten
1 cup boiling water	2 cups buttermilk
½ cup oil	1½ cups flour
⅓ cup brown sugar	2½ teaspoons soda
⅓ granulated sugar	½ teaspoon salt

Preheat the oven to 375 degrees. Mix bran and water and let stand for 20 minutes. Mix oil, sugars and eggs together and add to bran mixture. Sift dry ingredients and alternate adding the dry and buttermilk to the oil mixture. Portion batter evenly into a 12-cup muffin tray and bake for 15 minutes. Cool 5 minutes and invert.

Remember cooking is fun if it doesn't include much clean-up. Try out the new silicone and glass bakeware—you will be impressed.

Pumpkin Dessert Bread

3 cups all-purpose flour	1 cup brown sugar
1 teaspoon soda	2 cups canned pumpkin
1 teaspoon salt	4 eggs, beaten
3 teaspoons cinnamon	1¼ cups olive oil
1 cup granulated sugar	½ cup chopped nuts (optional)

Preheat the oven to 350 degrees. Place dry ingredients in a large mixing bowl. Make a deep well in the center. Mix remaining ingredients and pour into the well. Stir carefully, just enough to dampen ingredients. Pour into 2 prepared loaf pans. Bake for 60 minutes.

This recipe comes from a dear friend. Linda and I taught a culinary class in Fayetteville, North Carolina and this was one of our bakery items.

Simply Perfect Pastry Dough

4	cups flour		1¾	cups shortening
1	teaspoon baking powder		1	egg
1	tablespoon sugar		1	teaspoon vinegar
1	teaspoon salt		½	cup water

Mix the dry ingredients in mixing bowl and cut shortening into mixture. Mixture should resemble cornmeal. Mix remaining ingredients in large measuring cup and add to flour mixture. Bring into a ball and roll out onto a non-stick surface. Place in baking dish and fill with pie filling.

When making this crust for a pudding pie, poke holes in the bottom and sides with fork and bake at 425 degrees for 12 to 15 minutes.

This recipe is similar to my mother-in-law Lyla's pie recipe. I wanted something that was fool-proof and tastes marvelous and this is it. You will love it.

If you need help, just email and I will give you pointers on any of the recipes. When we created this book we wanted our customers to be able to ask questions.

Simply Sheila Rae Bread

3	cups bread flour	3	tablespoons olive oil
1	tablespoon commercial yeast	2	teaspoons salt
¼	cup granulated sugar	1	cup warm water

Using a large standing mixer place the flour, yeast, sugar, oil and salt. Start mixer and add a slow stream of water until all dry ingredients are incorporated. The dough should be sticky but not wet. Mix for about one minute. Shut off the machine and cover with cloth. Let rest for a ½ hour to 6 hours depending on your need. Form into rolls.

Whole wheat, rice, tapioca, potato flour can all work just mix and match. You must use at least 1 ½ cups of wheat based flour, this provides the necessary gluten to make a tender bread.

Commercial yeast can be purchased at bakeries or commercial food stores across the country.

Warm water activates the yeast, but it is better to be on the cooler end than the hotter. Hot water will kill the yeast and you can not bring it back to life. Water is also an item that must be added slowly, because humidity and temperature affect the actual amount. But it is approximately ⅓ cup water for every cup of flour.

If you are going to use it later in the day, note two things, if you live in hot climate refrigerate; covered and remove from the refrigerator ½ hour before using. If you live in cool climate leave on the counter; covered.

Have a question? Link onto my website at sheilaraellc.com.

Tropical Muffins

1 (10-ounce) jar maraschino cherries, drained
2 tablespoons maraschino juice
1¾ cups all-purpose flour
2 teaspoons baking powder
½ teaspoon salt

⅓ cup butter or margarine, softened
⅔ cup brown sugar
2 eggs, beaten
1 cup ripe bananas, mashed
½ cup macadamia nuts, chopped

Preheat the oven to 350 degrees. Drain cherries and cut cherries in quarters and set aside. Sift flour, baking powder and salt and set aside. In a medium mixing bowl, combine butter, brown sugar, eggs and cherry juice and mix on medium speed of electric mixer until ingredients are thoroughly combined. Add flour mixture and mashed bananas alternately, beginning and ending with flour mixture. Stir in cherries and nuts. Portion batter evenly into a 12-cup muffin tray and bake for 20 to 30 minutes or until golden brown and wooden pick inserted near center comes out clean.

Check out my website for great cooking ideas. Sheilaraellc.com.

SIMPLY FOR
KIDS

Andrew Bars

1	cup sugar	3	cups rice cereal
1	cup corn syrup	3	cups cornflakes, crushed
2½	cups peanut butter, divided	1	cup chocolate chips

In microwave safe dish, heat sugar and corn syrup to a boil. Add 1½ cups peanut butter and stir well. Add cereals. Pour into buttered 9x13x2-inch pan. Heat 1 cup peanut butter for 2 minutes in the microwave. Add chocolate chips and stir until melted. Frost the bars.

This recipe is our good friend Andrew's favorite. We started calling them Andrew bars after one of his visits.

Craziest Cake of All

2	cups flour	½	cup olive oil
½	teaspoon baking soda	1½	teaspoons vinegar
½	teaspoon salt	1	teaspoon vanilla
1⅓	cups sugar	1½	cups warm water
¼	cup cocoa		

Preheat the oven to 325 degrees. Combine dry ingredients in a 9x13-inch pan. Mix liquid ingredients in large measuring cup. Mix well. Pour over dry ingredients and whisk. Stir until all dry ingredients are combined. Bake for 35 to 40 minutes. Cool.

This cake is an all time favorite of mine because you don't have much to clean up. Personally, I use my 3-quart flexible mold and invert when cool and then frost with chocolate frosting.

Creamed Green Beans

2	(15-ounce) cans green beans		2	tablespoons flour
1	cup cream		3	tablespoons milk
1	teaspoon salt			

In a saucepan mix green beans, cream and salt. Over low heat cook beans for 20 minutes. Combine flour and milk and add green beans. Simmer until thickened.

This is probably my children's favorite side dish. My mother, Marlene, got the recipe from her mother. It was made for every holiday I can remember.

Dad's Chocolate Chip Pancakes

1½	cups milk		2	tablespoons sugar
2	tablespoons vinegar		1	teaspoon baking powder
3	eggs, beaten		1	teaspoon soda
3	tablespoons butter		½	teaspoon salt
1½	cups flour		1	cup chocolate chips

Mix milk and vinegar together and let set 5 minutes and add eggs and butter. Mix flour, sugar, baking powder, soda and salt in a separate bowl. Combine the dry and wet ingredients. DO NOT OVER STIR. Turn griddle on high. Scoop onto griddle and add a few chocolate chips. Turn pancakes as soon as they are puffed and full of bubbles.

This is my kids favorite "Dad" breakfast.

Easy Tex-Mex Bake

3 cups angel hair pasta, cooked
1 pound turkey breasts, ground, browned
⅔ cup medium salsa
1 (10-ounce) package frozen corn, thawed and drained
1 (15-ounce) can black beans, drained

1 (16-ounce) carton low fat cottage cheese
1 egg, beaten
1 tablespoon fresh cilantro
½ teaspoon pepper
¼ teaspoon cumin, ground
½ cup Monterey Jack cheese, shredded

Preheat the oven to 375 degrees. In a 2-quart baking dish place the pasta, turkey, salsa, beans and corn. In another bowl combine cottage cheese, egg, cilantro, pepper and cumin. Pour over turkey mixture, stirring slightly. Sprinkle with cheese. Bake for 20 minutes or until heated through and cheese is melted.

This is a great dish for the microwave; just heat for 12 minutes stirring every 3 minutes.

Elizabeth's Crispy Peanut Butter Cookies

1 cup crunchy peanut butter
1 cup brown sugar
1 teaspoon baking soda

1 egg, beaten
¼ cup peanuts, finely chopped

Preheat the oven to 350 degrees. Mix all ingredients until well incorporated and scoop dough onto a non-stick lined baking sheet. Bake for 15 minutes.

Give your kids the opportunity to bake with you. They will love it and you will appreciate your time together.

Fruit Filled Punch

2 (12-ounce) cans frozen lemonade
6 cups water
1 cup sugar

2 (1-liter) bottles ginger ale
1 (2-quart) container orange sherbet

Mix lemonade, water and sugar together. Add ginger ale and sherbet in punch bowl.

Ginger Snap Cookies

4 cups flour
2 teaspoons soda
5 teaspoons pumpkin pie spice
1 teaspoon salt
1⅓ cups shortening

2 cups sugar
2 eggs
½ cup molasses
1 teaspoon vanilla

Preheat the oven to 350 degrees. Sift flour, soda, spices and salt. Cream the shortening, sugar, eggs, molasses and vanilla. Mix dry ingredients in shortening mixture. Roll into balls and roll them in sugar. Place on a non-stick lined baking sheet. Bake for 10 minutes.

Grandma's Goulash

2	cups uncooked macaroni noodles	1	tablespoon dried onion
4	cups tomato juice	1	teaspoon salt
1	pound hamburger, browned	2	teaspoons chili powder

Preheat the oven to 350 degrees. In a 2-quart baking dish, mix all ingredients and bake 30 minutes or until noodles are done.

If you are not using a non-stick mold you will need to spray the pan well.

Homemade Strawberry Jam

| 8 | cups strawberries, mashed | 2 | tablespoons lemon juice |
| 6 | cups sugar, divided | | |

Put 4 cups sugar and strawberries in large saucepan. Boil over medium heat for 2 minutes. Add remaining sugar and boil 5 more minutes. Add lemon juice. Pour into prepared jelly jars. Cover and refrigerate.

This is a great family project. We go strawberry picking and then make it as a family.

Jiffy Bars

1	(9-ounce) box yellow cake mix	½	cup chopped walnuts
¼	cup brown sugar	1	egg
1	tablespoon butter	1	tablespoon water
1	tablespoon corn syrup	2	tablespoons flour
¼	cup chocolate chips		

Preheat the oven to 350 degrees. Blend all ingredients well in a mixing bowl and spread into a 9-inch baking dish. Bake for 25 to 30 minutes. Cool and cut.

Monkey Around Bread

4	(10-ounce) tubes buttermilk biscuits	½	cup butter
1	cup sugar	2	tablespoons milk
1	teaspoon cinnamon	1	teaspoon vanilla extract
1	cup brown sugar		

Preheat the oven to 350 degrees. Cut each biscuit into 4 pieces. Mix sugar and cinnamon in large plastic bag and add cut biscuits; shake to coat. Place into a Bundt pan. In a saucepan mix brown sugar, butter and milk and bring to boil. Remove from heat and add vanilla. Pour over biscuits. Bake for 30 minutes. Let cool 5 minutes and invert onto serving platter.

I do not say to spray pans in my recipes because I use a silicone coated glass pan. No sprays are needed because nothing sticks. If you want more information just check out my website at Sheilaraellc.com.

Pizza Burgers

1 pound ground lunch meat	1 teaspoon oregano
2 pounds hamburger, browned	2 tablespoons parsley
1 (16-ounce) jar spaghetti sauce	12 hamburger buns, halved
1½ cups mozzarella cheese, shredded	

Preheat the oven to 350 degrees. Combine lunch meat, hamburger, sauce, cheese and seasonings. Spread on top of each hamburger bun half. Toast in oven for 10 minutes.

Popcorn Balls

1 cup corn syrup	1 (3-ounce) package red gelatin
½ cup sugar	36 cups popcorn

Combine syrup and sugar and bring to a boil. Remove from heat and add gelatin; allow to dissolve. Pour thin stream over slightly salted popcorn. Stir to coat. Form into balls. Moisten hands to avoid sticking. Allow to dry and wrap in plastic wrap.

My great aunt and uncle drove a school bus for Elkton Public Schools. They would give each of their passengers one of these special popcorn balls for Christmas every year. What a great memory.

Rhubarb Punch

20 cups rhubarb, cut up
12 cups water
1 (12-ounce) can frozen orange juice
1 (12-ounce) can frozen lemon juice

2 (3-ounce) packages strawberry gelatin
4 cups sugar
1 (46-ounce) bottle pineapple juice
1 (1-liter) bottle lemon-lime soda

Cook rhubarb and water until tender; strain juice well. Mix orange, lemon and rhubarb juice together with sugar and bring to a boil. Add gelatin. Cool. Add pineapple juice and soda.

Roasted Asparagus

1½ pounds thin asparagus
2½ tablespoons extra-virgin olive oil
½ teaspoon sea salt

⅛ teaspoon fresh ground pepper
⅓ cup fresh Parmesan cheese

Preheat the oven to 450 degrees. On a non-stick lined baking sheet toss asparagus, oil, salt and pepper. Roast 15 minutes and transfer to serving platter and add cheese.

I love sea salt for roasting; it adds a crisp fresh flavor.

You could roast many different vegetables by using the same ingredients.

Scalloped Corn

2	(15-ounce) cans cream style corn	½	teaspoon salt
¾	cup milk	¼	teaspoon pepper
1	cup soda crackers, crushed	2	eggs, beaten

Preheat the oven to 350 degrees. In a 2-quart baking dish mix all ingredients and bake for 1 hour.

Sheila Rae's Simple Pizza for Kids

1	batch Sheila Rae's Simple Bread	½	cup onions
1	cup spaghetti sauce	½	cup bacon, pieces
½	cup sausage, cooked	2	cups cheese
½	cup pepperoni		

Preheat the oven to 400 degrees. On a non-stick sheet liner roll ½ the dough out thin. Slide non-stick liner onto perforated pan. Top with your favorite toppings. Repeat with the rest of the dough. Bake 20 minutes or until cheese is melted.

This is great for birthday partys because kids can create their own masterpieces.

Speedy Vegetarian Lasagna

1   (26-ounce) jar tomato sauce
6   no-boil, oven-ready lasagna noodles
1   (12-ounce) package soy Tofu
    crumbles
1   (8-ounce) package ready-to-use
    mushrooms, sliced

⅔ cup mozzarella cheese, finely
    shredded
3   tablespoons Parmesan cheese,
    grated

Preheat the oven to 400 degrees. Put ½ cup pasta sauce into a 2-quart baking dish, tilting to spread. Layer 2 lasagna noodles over the sauce, break to fit and alternate a ½ package of the meatless crumbles over noodles, ½ of the package of the mushrooms and ⅓ cup mozzarella cheese. Press lightly to flatten. Repeat using the remaining ingredient. Finish with the last 2 noodles and sauce. Cover with aluminum foil and bake for 30 minutes. Remove foil and add Parmesan cheese; place back in oven for 5 minutes.

Cooking is fun. My children are responsible for one supper one day a week. They learn responsibility, how to read a recipe, how to figure fractions and the importance of following directions.

Turtles

¼	pound almond bark, chopped	36	caramels
¼	pound chocolate bark, chopped	1	(16-ounce) bag pecan halves

Preheat the oven to 300 degrees. On a non-stick baking sheet place 4 pecan halves for the legs and lay one caramel and flatten slightly. Heat in oven for 2 minutes then push caramels down onto pecans. Melt chocolates in the microwave for 1 minute and stir well. Place small amount of chocolates onto each caramel. Cool.

Zachery's Bagel Pizza

4	bagels, split	32	pepperoni slices
½	cup pizza sauce	1½	cups mozzarella cheese

Preheat the oven to 400 degrees. Place 8 bagel halves onto a non-stick lined baking sheet and spread sauce on top of each. Top with 4 pepperonis and sprinkle with cheese. Bake 8 minutes or until golden brown.

SIMPLY SWEET

Candy and Frostings

Almond Brittle

2	cups sugar	1	teaspoon baking soda
½	cup water	1	cup raw almonds, sliced
3	tablespoons butter, softened		

Mix the sugar, water and almonds in a 2-quart mold. Microwave 3 minutes and stir for 3 minutes stir, 2 minutes stir, 2 minutes stir, 1 minute stir, and 1 minute stir. Add soda and butter; stir well. Spread onto a non-stick lined baking sheet. Cool brittle. Break into large pieces.

This recipe is so easy but the first time you make it you need to watch for a caramel color between each stirring. The color will indicate it is done; some microwaves are much more powerful than others.

Best Frosting Ever

1	cup milk	1	cup granulated sugar
5	tablespoons flour	1	tablespoon vanilla
1	cup shortening	½	teaspoon salt

Mix the flour and milk in a heavy saucepan. Heat until thickened while stirring constantly. Cool. In large mixing bowl whip shortening, sugar, vanilla and salt until light, at least 5 minutes. When flour mixture is cool add to shortening mixture and whip at least 5 minutes.

This frosting is light and not overly sweet. My grandma always filled doughnuts with it. I use it to frost my children's birthday cakes.

Bing Bars

1	cup sugar	1	teaspoon vanilla
6	large marshmallows	¾	cup chocolate chips
⅓	cup evaporated milk	¾	cup peanut butter
⅛	teaspoon salt	1	cup salted peanuts
⅓	cup cherry chips		

Bring the sugar, marshmallows, evaporated milk and salt to a boil over medium heat. Once it starts to a boil start a timer for 1 minute. Add cherry chips and stir well. Pour into a 9x13x2-inch pan. Heat peanut butter in microwave for 2 minutes and add chocolate chips, vanilla and peanuts. Spread over first layer. Cool and cut.

Cherry chips are not common all over the country but can be located on the internet and are well worth the effort. I will help you if you email. sheilaraellc.com.

This recipe has been made by my family for years. There is a candy that reminds me of these that is sold in the upper Midwest and is manufactured in Sioux City, Iowa.

Butter Cream Frosting

½	cup vegetable shortening	1	teaspoon salt
½	cup butter	4	cups sifted powdered sugar
1	teaspoon vanilla extract	2	tablespoons milk

Cream butter, shortening, vanilla, and salt for 3 minutes and add powdered sugar 1 cup at a time. If icing is too thick or appears dry add 1 tablespoon of milk at a time. Keep frosting covered with damp cloth until ready to use.

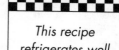

This recipe refrigerates well in an airtight container.

Salt is what makes this recipe very good; without it, it is too sweet.

Butter Crunch Toffee

1 cup salted butter	½ cup chopped pecans
1½ cups sugar	1 (16-ounce) package chocolate chips
3 tablespoons water	½ cup toasted almond
1 tablespoon corn syrup	½ cup toasted pecans
½ cup chopped almonds	

In a large saucepan melt butter then add sugar, water and corn syrup. Cook over medium heat, stirring occasionally to hard crack stage (300 degrees). Quickly stir in first ½ of pecans and almonds. Spread onto a non-stick lined baking sheet. Top with chocolate chips. Let stand for 5 minutes. Spread chocolate evenly over the candy. Sprinkle with toasted almonds and pecans. Cool.

For the hard crack stage take candy to 300 degrees and then let it boil for one additional minute. This minute improves the overall crunch of this candy.

I like to mix different nuts and find that pecans and the almonds are my families' favorite, but I also like walnuts and cashews.

Candy is not that hard to make, but you do need a good candy thermometer. Email sheilaraellc.com for suggestions.

Caramel Candy

2 cups white sugar	1 ½ cups light corn syrup
1 cup butter	2 cups cream, divided

Place ½ the cream, sugar, butter and syrup into a 4-quart saucepan. Heat slowly, stirring constantly until mixture boils and reaches 260 degrees; remove from heat and add vanilla and the other cup of cream. Pour into a 9x13x2-inch pan or individual candy molds.

Purchase a good quality candy thermometer before making any candy to ensure quality.

Make sure you butter baking dishes very well if you are not using a non-stick flexible mold.

This recipe comes from a family friend, Darlene Bauer. I was fortunate enough one evening to have a private lesson on how to make her fabulous candy.

Cheese Fudge

1 cup butter	2 pounds powdered sugar
½ pound Velveeta cheese	1 tablespoon vanilla
½ cup cocoa	1 cup chopped nuts

Melt cheese and butter and add sugar, cocoa, vanilla and nuts and mix well. Pour into a 2-quart baking dish.

I always use flexible molds when I am making candy. See the front of the book for further information.

This recipe comes from my dear friend Debbie Wilcox. Sounds a little funny with cheese and chocolate but I guarantee you and your family will enjoy.

Chewing Cinnamon Candies

1	(16-ounce) package marshmallows	½	teaspoon salt
1	(9-ounce) bag red hot candies	2½	cups rice cereal
3	tablespoons butter		

In a large mixing bowl melt butter and add marshmallow and red hot candies. Microwave at 50 percent power. Stir every 2 minutes until smooth. Add cereal, working quickly. Pour onto a non-stick surface. Cool. Cut. Dust with powdered sugar.

These candies are very sticky so use as many non-stick products that you can to lessen your clean-up efforts.

Chocolate Chip Frosting

⅓	cup milk	¼	cup butter
1	cup sugar	½	cup chocolate chips

Heat milk, sugar and butter in microwave for 3 minutes or until it comes to a boil. Boil for 1 minute and add chocolate chips. Stir and allow to cool 3 to 5 minutes before frosting.

Easiest Dark Fudge Ever

2¼ cups chocolate chips
1 (14-ounce) can sweetened
    condensed milk

1 teaspoon vanilla extract
1 teaspoon almond extract
⅓ cup chopped walnuts

Heat sweetened condensed milk in microwave for 3 minutes. Add chocolate, extracts, and walnuts. Mix well and pour into a 2-quart non-stick baking dish. Cool.

Replace with another flavor of chips.

I love to make this recipe in my silicone and glass flower mold. When it cools I cut it into 4 equal parts and it looks like 4 individual hearts. I then wrap them up in pretty cellophane and give them as gifts.

Easy Chewing Caramels

1 (14-ounce) bag caramels
3 tablespoons cream
2 cups walnut pieces

1 teaspoon butter
1 pound chocolate coating

In a microwave safe bowl, melt caramels and cream at 50 percent power, making sure to stir after each minute until smooth then add nuts. Pour into non-stick candy molds. Chill. Melt chocolate in microwave for 1 minute, making sure to stir between each minute. Dip in chocolate and place back on non-stick surface. Chill.

There are neat dispensers on the market that look like pancake batter dispensers but are smaller. These allow for easy candy making. If you would like information on the non-stick candy molds or the dispenser just email me. sheilaraellc.com.

Jalapeño Peanut Brittle

3	jalapeños, chopped	3	cups peanuts
⅓	cup water	1	teaspoon salt
2	cups sugar	2	teaspoons butter
1	cup light corn syrup	2	teaspoons baking soda

In a glass measuring cup place jalapeño and water and microwave for 5 minutes. Let stand for 15 minutes. Drain and reserve liquid and discard jalapeños. In a large non-stick saucepan mix sugar, jalapeño liquid and syrup, making sure to mix well. Stir over medium heat until candy thermometer reaches 240 degrees and add peanuts. Continue stirring until candy reaches 298 degrees and remove from heat and add salt, butter and baking soda; stir well. Pour onto a non-stick baking sheet and let cool completely; break into bite-size pieces.

This is a great recipe for people who like a little spice in their life.

If you use non-stick silicone baking sheet liners you do not have to butter it and it improves the quality of the product.

Mints

1	(3-ounce) package cream cheese	3	cups powdered sugar
½	teaspoon flavoring, your choice		

Soften cream cheese and add flavoring; mix well. Add powdered sugar and mix well. Form balls and roll in sugar and press into flexible candy molds. Chill.

Dip mints in melted white or dark chocolate.

This was a family affair before any wedding, my aunts would roll and the cousins would mold in to roses and hearts. I remember this as being a very fun time growing up. This is a great family memory. Make memories of your own.

Peanut Brittle

1 cup corn syrup	1 teaspoon salt
⅓ cup water	2 teaspoons baking soda
2 cups sugar	2 teaspoons butter
3 cups peanuts	

Bring the corn syrup, water and sugar to a boil and cook until candy thermometer reaches 240 degrees then add the peanuts and return to the heat. Cook to 295 degrees and remove from heat and add the salt, baking soda and butter. Pour onto a non-stick lined baking sheet.

If you like caramel popcorn you can pour this mixture over 8 cups of popcorn.

Peanut Butter Balls

1½ cups crushed graham crackers	1 tablespoon vanilla
1 cup butter, softened	1½ cups peanut butter
1 pound powdered sugar	1 (16-ounce) block chocolate coating

Mix all ingredients except chocolate coating in a large mixer; mix well. Form into walnut-size pieces and freeze. Melt chocolate coating. Dip candies into coating and place on a non-stick lined baking sheet. Let glaze harden.

Seven-Minute White Icing

2   egg whites
1½ cups sugar
5   tablespoons cold water

¼   cup cream of tartar
1   teaspoon vanilla

Place all the ingredients, except for the flavoring, in the top of a double boiler. Beat until they are thoroughly blended. Place top over bottom of double boiler filled with rapidly boiling water. Beat icing with wire whisk for 7 minutes. Remove from heat and add flavoring. Let cool slightly.

For nut icing you can add ½ cup chopped nut meats to cooked icing.

For Lemon Icing use only 2 tablespoons water and add 2 tablespoons lemon juice and ¼ teaspoon grated lemon rind.

For orange icing omit water and add ½ teaspoon grated orange rind and ¼ cup orange juice.

For chocolate icing melt 3-ounces chocolate in microwave for 1 minute or until melted; when icing is cooked fold-in vanilla and melted chocolate.

For coconut icing first spread the cooked icing on the cake and sprinkle with shredded coconut.

Sour Cream Frosting

1   cup sour cream

½   cup chocolate chips

Heat the sour cream in microwave for 2 minutes and add chocolate chips. Stir well.

SIMPLY SWEET

Cookies

Aunt Sally's Ginger Cookies

1	cup sugar	1	teaspoon salt
1	cup butter	2	teaspoons soda
2	eggs	4½	cups flour
1	cup molasses	1	egg white, room temperature
1	cup cold coffee	1	cup sugar
1	teaspoon cinnamon	⅓	cup water
1	teaspoon ginger		

Preheat the oven to 350 degrees. Cream sugar and butter then add eggs, molasses and coffee. Sift together all dry ingredients and add to butter mixture then mix well. Scoop by heaping teaspoons onto a non-stick lined cookie sheet. Bake 10 to 12 minutes. Cool. Microwave sugar and water for 2 minutes, stir and repeat, stir again and microwave 30 more seconds. Beat egg white until frothy stage and slowly add syrup in three stages. Whip well between each addition and beat an additional 2 minutes. Frost the cookies.

This is a real crowd pleaser and my son Zachery's favorite cookie.

Black Forest Bars

1	package chocolate cake mix	1	(10-ounce) package frozen sour cherries, thawed
4	eggs	1	(3-ounce) package cherry gelatin
⅔	cup butter, melted		

Frost with thin powdered sugar glaze or whipped topping.

Preheat the oven to 325 degrees. Mix all ingredients together. Pour into a jelly-roll pan lined with a non-stick baking sheet. Bake for 30 to 35 minutes.

Butter Cookies

1 cup butter	1 teaspoon baking soda
1 cup powdered sugar	1 teaspoon cream of tartar
1 egg	1 teaspoon vanilla
2 cups flour	¼ teaspoon salt

Preheat the oven to 350 degrees. Cream butter and powdered sugar for 2 minutes and then stir in the rest of ingredients. Roll into balls. Place on a non-stick lined baking sheet. Press down with damp glass dipped in sugar. Bake for 10 to 12 minutes.

I always use a pretty bottom glass to make an elegant impression.

Cheesecake Cookies

1 cup butter, softened	1 cup brown sugar
1 (8-ounce) package cream cheese, softened	1 teaspoon vanilla
1 cup granulated sugar	2 cups flour
	½ cup chocolate chips

Preheat the oven to 375 degrees. Cream butter, cream cheese, vanilla and sugars together and add flour and chips. Scoop onto a non-stick lined baking sheet. Bake for 12 to 13 minutes. Cool before removing from pan.

These are best cool.

This recipe comes from our friends the Womble's in North Carolina. Their oldest daughter loved to make them and share with us.

Chocolate Coffee Bean Biscotti

1	package white cake mix	2	large eggs
½	cup ground chocolate covered coffee beans	½	cup olive oil
		½	cup chopped almonds
¾	cup flour	2	tablespoons water
¼	cup cocoa		

Preheat the oven to 350 degrees. Mix dry ingredients in one bowl and wet ingredients in another. Incorporate the wet ingredients into the dry. Shape into two 10x4-inch oblong shapes on non-stick surface. Bake for 15 minutes. Cool 10 minutes. Cut each oblong into 10 cookies and place them on their sides on a non-stick lined cookie sheet and bake for an additional 10 minutes. Cool.

These cookies are simple to make but are difficult to stir; I recommend a standing mixer to help you out.

Chocolate Crinkle Cookies

1	package chocolate cake mix	½	cup plain yogurt
2	eggs	½	cup powdered sugar

Preheat the oven to 350. Mix cake mix, eggs and yogurt together. Drop by teaspoons into powdered sugar and coat. Place on a non-stick lined baking sheet and bake for 8 to 10 minutes. Cool on the pan for 2 minutes. Move to cooling rack.

When I taught school my students were always excited when I decided to bake for them and this was one of their favorite recipes.

Cookies While You Sleep

2   eggs, room temperature
⅔   cup sugar
½   teaspoon almond extract

1   teaspoon vanilla
1   cup chocolate chips
1   cup walnuts

Preheat the oven to 350 degrees. Beat egg whites until stiff peaks form. Gradually add the sugar and beat until very stiff. Add the almond and vanilla flavoring and fold in the chocolate chips and walnuts. Drop by teaspoons on non-stick lined baking sheet. Place in oven and then turn off oven. Leave cookies in the oven overnight.

Corn Flake Drops

3   egg whites, room temperature
1½ cups sugar
⅛   teaspoon cream of tartar
4   cups corn flakes, crushed

½   cup nut meats
½   cup shredded coconut
1   teaspoon vanilla

Preheat the oven to 325 degrees. Beat egg whites until stiff and add sugar and cream of tartar slowly then fold in remaining ingredients. Drop batter by teaspoons onto a non-stick lined baking sheet. Bake for 9 to 11 minutes.

Crisp Cookies

1 cup sugar
1 cup brown sugar
1 cup shortening
1 egg
1 cup oil
1 cup oatmeal
2 teaspoons vanilla
1 cup rice cereal

3½ cups flour
1 teaspoon cream of tartar
1 teaspoon soda
½ teaspoon salt
½ teaspoon almond flavor
½ cup almonds, chopped
1 (12-ounce) package chocolate chips

Preheat the oven to 350 degrees. Cream sugars, shortening, and eggs and add the oil and vanilla. Sift dry ingredients and add to creamed mixture. Add cereal, almonds and chips. Scoop into ball and flatten lightly on non-stick lined baking sheet. Bake for 10 to 12 minutes.

Dark Chocolate Oatmeal Cookies

¾ cup flour
¼ cup unsweetened cocoa powder
½ teaspoon baking soda
¼ teaspoon salt
½ cup butter, room temperature

½ cup brown sugar
½ teaspoon vanilla extract
2 tablespoons oatmeal
¼ cup semi-sweet chocolate chips

Preheat the oven to 350 degrees. Sift flour, cocoa, baking soda and salt in a medium bowl. Using electric mixer beat butter until fluffy and add sugar and vanilla. Beat until blended then add flour mixture and beat until moist clumps form. Mix in oats with spatula until evenly distributed; dough will be very firm. Add chocolate chips and knead gently to blend. Scoop onto a non-stick lined baking sheet leaving a 2-inch space between cookies. Press down. Bake cookies until center is slightly firm and top is cracked, about 14 minutes. Cool on sheet.

Erik's Favorite Cookies

1 cup sugar	1 teaspoon soda
1 cup brown sugar	2 teaspoons baking powder
1½ cups butter	3 cups quick oatmeal
2 eggs	1 cup corn flakes, crushed
2½ cups flour	2 cups butterscotch chips

Preheat the oven to 375 degrees. Cream together sugars, butter and add eggs. Mix flour, soda, baking powder together and add to butter mixture. Stir in oatmeal, corn flakes and chips. Scoop cookies onto a non-stick lined baking sheet and bake for 10 minutes.

I use a number 40 cookie scoop for making these cookies; it makes them a nice size and uniform.

Grandma Jorenby's Famous Date Cookies

1 (10-ounce) package dates, chopped	2 cups brown sugar
½ cup water	1 cup shortening
½ cup granulated sugar	2 eggs
1 teaspoon soda	3½ cups flour
2 tablespoons hot water	⅛ teaspoon salt

Preheat the oven to 375 degrees. Mix dates, water and granulated sugar together in the microwave for one minute; stir; repeat two more times. Let cool. Mix soda and hot water; let dissolve. Cream brown sugar and shortening and add eggs, water mixture, salt and flour. Form cookie mixture into a 1-inch ball; make a thumb imprint in the center on a non-stick lined baking sheet. Place a heaping ¼ teaspoon of date mixture into imprint. Top with a small amount of dough. Repeat and bake for 8 to 10 minutes.

This recipe came from a very special lady in my life, my Grandma Jorenby. She was a marvelous cook and friend.

Grandma Landsman's Filled Sandwich Cookies

1¼ cups butter, divided
⅓ cup sour cream
2 cups flour
½ teaspoon salt, divided

1½ teaspoons vanilla, divided
¾ cup powdered sugar
1 egg yolk
¼ teaspoon salt

Preheat the oven to 350 degrees. Cream butter, sour cream, ¼ teaspoon salt, ½ teaspoon vanilla and stir in flour. Chill. Cut into eight equal parts. Work with one part at a time and chill remaining dough. Roll dough into ⅛-inch sheet using sugar on your work surface. The sugar will prevent it from sticking and adds the crunch to the cookies. Cut into 1-inch circles. Prick with fork and place on non-stick lined baking sheet. Bake 8 to 10 minutes until golden brown. Cool. Make filling with ¼ cup butter, powdered sugar, 1 egg yolk, 1 teaspoon vanilla and ¼ teaspoon salt. Place small amount of filling between two cookies to form sandwich cookies.

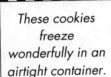

These cookies freeze wonderfully in an airtight container.

The egg yolk can be left out of the filling recipe and replaced with a small amount of water.

This is my favorite cookie recipe from Grandma Landsman. She is an amazing baker who taught me to cook by "feel". She is a wonderful woman who I am so thankful is part of my life.

Lemon Ripple Cheesecake Bars

1 cup all-purpose flour	3 (8-ounce) packages cream cheese
¼ cup sugar	3 eggs
1 teaspoon finely grated lemon zest	1 (14-ounce) can sweetened
⅛ teaspoon salt	condensed milk
½ cup butter, cut into ½-inch pieces and chilled	

Preheat the oven to 325 degrees and position a rack in the center. In a food processor pulse the flour with the sugar, lemon zest and salt; add the butter and pulse until a soft, crumbly dough forms. Press the dough evenly over the bottom and up the side of a 9x13x2-inch cake pan. Bake the crust for 20 minutes, or until golden and firm.

Mix cream cheese and sweetened condensed milk and mix well then add eggs. Pour the cream cheese batter over the crust and smooth the surface with a spatula. Bake the cheesecake for about 60 minutes in a water bath. Let cool on a wire rack for 1 hour and then refrigerate until thoroughly chilled. Unmold and cut.

A water bath improves the moisture in cheesecake and I normally bake all cheesecakes and custards in them. If you need more information just email me. sheilaraellc.com.

Mom's Sugar Cookies

½ teaspoon baking powder	2 eggs
3 cups flour	1 cup sugar
1 cup butter	1 teaspoon vanilla

Preheat the oven to 375 degrees. Cut butter into flour. Beat eggs, sugar, and vanilla for 3 to 5 minutes. Stir egg mixture into the flour mixture. DO NOT over work. Working with small batches at a time roll and cut into your favorite shapes. Bake 8 to 10 minutes on a non-stick lined baking sheet. Cool.

This is another recipe from my mom Marlene. These are wonderful cookies that actually get better as they set. My mother stores them in an airtight container and refrigerates.

My family likes them frosted with butter cream frosting.

No Bake Butterscotch Pudding Cookies

2 cups brown sugar	1 (3.4-ounce) instant butterscotch pudding
¾ cup butter	
3½ cups oatmeal	

Melt butter and sugar and bring to a boil in the microwave. Add instant butterscotch pudding and oatmeal. Let sit for 15 minutes and drop by spoonfuls onto a non-stick lined baking sheet. Cool.

Nutty Squares

6	tablespoons granulated sugar	¼	cup light corn syrup
4	tablespoons butter, divided	⅓	cup butterscotch chips
1	teaspoon vanilla	⅓	cup white chocolate chips
1	egg yolk	1	cup mixed nuts, chopped
1	cup baking mix		

Preheat the oven to 350 degrees. Mix sugar, 3 tablespoons butter, vanilla and yolk together and add baking mix. Press into a 1-quart baking dish. Bake until brown and cool. Mix corn syrup, 1 tablespoon butter and heat in microwave for 1 minute or until it boils. Add chips. Cool 3 minutes and spread over first layer. Top with nuts. Refrigerate for 1 hour. Cut into 1-inch squares.

My friend Dianna loves to try new recipes and this one came from her; it has become one of my favorite bars.

Tasty Cream Cheese Bars

1	package chocolate cake mix	1	cup chocolate chips
3	eggs	1	(8-ounce) package cream cheese
½	cup butter	1	pound powdered sugar
1	cup walnuts, chopped	1	teaspoon vanilla

Preheat the oven to 350 degrees. Mix cake mix, 1 egg, butter, walnuts and chocolate chips together and press into a 9x13x2-inch pan. In a large mixing bowl whip 2 eggs, cream cheese, powdered sugar and vanilla. Pour over first layer. Bake for 40 minutes. Remove from oven and allow cooling.

Do not over bake. I always remove at 40 minutes.

SIMPLY
SWEET

Desserts

Brown Sugar Baked Apples

8	large Granny Smith apples	6	tablespoons pure maple syrup
½	cup packed dark brown sugar	4	tablespoons butter, cut into small pieces
1	teaspoon cinnamon, ground		
½	teaspoon nutmeg, ground		

Preheat the oven to 350 degrees. Peel skin off top quarter of each apple. Remove the core, leaving bottom intact. Stand apples in a large non-stick mold. Mix sugar and spices in a bowl and reserve 2 tablespoons of mixture. Fill apple cavities with remaining sugar mixture. Spoon ½ tablespoon of maple syrup into each cavity. Scatter 3 tablespoons butter pieces over apples. Pour ½ cup water into pan with apples. Bake apples for 35 minutes. Add reserved 2 tablespoons maple syrup, 1 tablespoon butter and ½ cup water to pan. Bake until apples are tender when pierced with skewer, about 25 minutes longer. Transfer apples to 8 bowls. Pour reserved liquid into small saucepan and reduce for 5 minutes over medium heat. Spoon the sauce over apples. Serve with whipping cream if desired.

Brown Sugar Pound Cake with Caramel Sauce

1½ cups butter, softened, divided	½ teaspoon baking powder
2½ cups brown sugar, divided	1 cup half-and-half
1½ cups granulated sugar, divided	3 tablespoons vanilla, divided
6 large eggs	½ cup whipping cream
3 cups all-purpose flour	1 tablespoon light corn syrup
¾ teaspoon salt	

Preheat the oven to 325 degrees. Cream 1 cup butter, 2 cups brown sugar and 1 cup granulated sugar and heat until very light and fluffy. Add eggs one at a time, beating well after each addition. Combine dry ingredients and add to batter alternately with half-and-half, beginning and ending with the flour mixture. Add 2 tablespoons vanilla. Fill a 2-quart baking dish and bake for 1 hour and 35 to 40 minutes or until toothpick inserted in center of cake comes out clean. Cool cake completely and remove from pan. To serve, drizzle with Caramel Sauce. For sauce combine cream, ½ cup butter, ½ cup brown sugar, ½ cup granulated sugar and corn syrup. Bring to a boil over medium heat, whisking occasionally. Cover and continue to boil for 1 minute and add 1 tablespoon vanilla. Uncover and boil for 3 to 4 minutes without stirring. Cool slightly and drizzle over cake.

Chocolate Chiffon Dessert

1 cup chopped walnuts	½ cup sugar, divided
½ cup chocolate chip cookies, crushed	¼ teaspoon salt
1 envelope unflavored gelatin	½ cup cream
¼ cup cold water	3 eggs, separated
1 ½ cups semi-sweet chocolate	1 cup cream, whipped

Mix chopped walnuts and cookie crumbs. Cover bottom 10- inch tart pan with ½ of mixture. Soften gelatin in cold water. Heat milk, ¼ cup sugar and salt in microwave and bring to a boil then add semi-sweet chocolate and stir until smooth. Beat egg yolks and add hot mixture slowly while stirring rapidly. Return to microwave; cook at 50% power, stirring every 30 seconds until thickened. Add gelatin; stir until dissolved. Chill until thickened. Beat egg whites until stiff and gradually add remaining ¼ cup sugar and beat very stiff. Fold in chocolate mixture and whipped cream. Pour over crumb crust and top with remaining crumb mixture. Chill until firm.

Chocolate Peppermint Cake

1 package white cake mix	1 (8½-ounce) package chocolate mint patties
½ cup oil	
1 ¼ cups water	1 cup heavy whipping cream
3 egg whites	

Preheat the oven to 325 degrees. Mix cake, oil, water and egg whites until smooth. Pour into prepared 2-quart baking dish. Bake 45 to 50 minutes or until cake tester comes out clean. Melt chocolate mint patties over hot water bath until smooth then cool. Whip cream and fold in melted mint patties.

This is a wonderful cake served warm with ice cream and a sprig of mint.

Coconut Sour Cream Cake

1¼ cups sour cream, divided
1 cup cream of coconut, divided
3 large eggs
¼ cup butter, melted

1 tablespoon fresh lemon juice
1 package white cake mix
2 cups flaked sweetened coconut, toasted, divided

Preheat the oven to 325 degrees. Combine 1 cup sour cream, ¾ cup cream of coconut, eggs, butter and lemon juice in a large bowl. Add white cake mix and 1 cup coconut and blend well. Pour into 3-quart baking dish.. Bake cake until top is golden brown and tester inserted into center comes out clean, about 50 minutes. Meanwhile, blend remaining ¼ cup sour cream and remaining ¼ cup cream of coconut in small bowl. Spread mixture evenly over warm cake. Return cake to oven and bake 5 minutes longer. Sprinkle coconut over. Place pan on rack and cool cake completely before removing from the pan.

This is a recipe I truly believe needs a non-stick mold and I can guarantee it will impress your pickiest critics. Check out the front of the book for more details.

Cream Cheese Pound Cake

1½ cups butter
1 (8-ounce) package cream cheese
2 cups sugar
1 cup brown sugar

½ teaspoon salt
2 teaspoons vanilla extract
6 large eggs
3 cups sifted cake flour

Preheat the oven to 325 degrees. Cream the margarine, cream cheese and sugar until light and fluffy. Add salt and vanilla and beat well. Add eggs, one at a time, beating after each addition. Stir in flour. Pour mixture into a 2-quart baking dish and bake for about 1½ hours or until cake tester comes out clean.

Use a cake tester every time. Do not wait for it to pull away from the edge of the pan; it will be over baked.

My friend and mentor, Debbie makes the best pound cakes and this is a variation of one of her recipes.

Custard Pie

½ cup sugar
4 tablespoons flour
4 eggs, beaten

2 cups half-and-half
2 teaspoons vanilla
1 (9-inch) graham cracker crust

Preheat the oven to 350 degrees. Mix flour and sugar together very well. Mix eggs, half-and-half and vanilla; add the sugar/flour combination. Pour into a graham cracker crust. Bake for 30 minutes.

Danish Pastry Pies

1 cup shortening
½ cup sour cream
1½ cups flour

½ teaspoon salt
1 (21-ounce) can of pie filling

Preheat the oven to 375 degrees. Mix shortening and cream together. Mix flour and salt together. Stir the mixtures together. Roll out onto a non-stick surface. Cut into 4-inch squares. Place 1 tablespoon filling in the center of each square. Fold from corner to corner. Press edges together to seal. Bake for 15 to 20 minutes.

Easy Lime Pie

⅓ cup lime juice
4 egg yolks

1 (14-ounce) can sweetened condensed milk
1 (9-inch) graham cracker pie crust

Preheat the oven to 250 degrees. Mix together lime juice, yolks and sweetened condensed milk. Pour into the crust. Bake for 20 minutes. Cool.

My high school students in Reading, Michigan made this recipe for a dessert auction and received $12.00 for it. The people who bought it could not have been more pleased. They told me afterwards it was one of the best pies they had ever had.

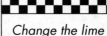

Change the lime juice to key lime or lemon.

Easy Pineapple Dessert

1 package white cake mix
1 (3.9-ounce) package instant vanilla pudding
1½ cups half-and-half
1 (8-ounce) package cream cheese, softened

½ cup cream
1 (20-ounce) can crushed pineapple, well drained
2 cups non-dairy whipped topping
½ cup toasted coconut

Preheat the oven to 325 degrees. Prepare cake mix according to box directions and bake in 9x13-inch pan for 30 to 35 minutes. Cool completely. Mix vanilla pudding and half-and-half. Spread onto cake. Mix cream cheese, cream and pineapple. Spread onto pudding layer. Frost dessert with whipped topping and sprinkle with coconut. Refrigerate overnight.

I love this cake done in my 3-quart mold (discussed in the front of the cookbook) and then sliced into 3 rounds and filled with the first topping and then completely frosted in the whipped topping and finally coated with coconut. It is a beautiful presentation.

Fast Sponge Cake Jelly Roll

1⅓ cups eggs
1⅓ cups sugar
1 teaspoon vanilla

½ teaspoon salt
1⅓ cups flour
½ cup jam

Preheat the oven to 375 degree. Place a non-stick liner in the bottom of a ¼ sheet cake pan. Beat together the eggs and sugar until fluffy. Add vanilla and salt. Slowly add the flour. Pour into prepared pan. Bake for 15 minutes. Cool completely. Invert onto a large cloth that is coated with sugar. Fill with jam. Roll up using the cloth to prevent the cake from breaking. Chill for 15 minutes before cutting.

If you didn't notice all the main ingredients are the same amount, you can make a bigger version by doing 1½ cups of eggs, sugar and flour, or a smaller version with 1 cup of eggs, sugar and flour. The other 2 ingredients do not have to be changed.

Anytime you are whipping eggs make sure that they are at room temperature.

Fresh Peach Pie

4	whole peaches, sliced	3	tablespoons cornstarch
1	cup crushed peaches	1	tablespoon butter
1	cup sugar	1	(9-inch) pie crust, baked

Combine sugar and cornstarch and stir in crushed peaches. Cook in microwave for 8 minutes or until filling is clear and add butter. Cool 5 minutes and add sliced peaches. Pour into pie shell. Chill for about 2 hours.

This same recipe can be used for making fresh strawberry pie. As a child this recipe was a favorite. I grew up in a family of 4 and my mom would cut this pie in fourth's and we could eat it as we wished but if it was still there at 4 a.m. when my father got up to milk cows, it was his.

Fruit Cake with Twist

1	yellow cake mix	1	(3.9-ounce) package instant vanilla pudding
½	cup vegetable oil		
1	(14-ounce) can Mandarin oranges with juice	1	(20-ounce) can of crushed pineapple and juice
4	eggs	1	(8-ounce) carton of Cool Whip

Preheat the oven to 350 degrees. Mix together the yellow cake mix, ½ cup oil and oranges and pour into two prepared 8-inch cake pans. Bake for 30 to 38 minutes. To make frosting, stir crushed pineapple into the vanilla pudding. Then fold in Cool Whip. Frost the cake.

My preference is to use a beautifully shaped mold. This cake is one that impresses family and friends at any occasion.

Fruit Up-Side Down Cake

¼	cup butter	1	cup sugar
¾	cup brown sugar	½	cup sour milk
1	cup pecan pieces	1	tablespoon shortening, melted
1	can peaches, drained	1	teaspoon vanilla
2	eggs	1	cup cake flour, sifted
¼	teaspoon salt	1	teaspoon baking powder

Melt the butter in a 2-quart baking dish. Sprinkle brown sugar and pecans over butter. Arrange fruit on sugar. To prepare the batter: Beat eggs until light. Add sugar and salt gradually, beating constantly. Heat the milk to boiling point. Add shortening. Beat into egg mixture. Add vanilla. Sift flour with baking powder, and add it to egg mixture. Beat quickly until blended. Pour batter over fruit. Bake cake in a moderate 325 degree oven for 40 minutes. Cool. Invert onto serving platter.

If you are in a rush, use a cake mix in place of the homemade cake and bake in the microwave for 10 to 14 minutes. Use the toothpick test to see if it is done.

Heavenly Pie

3	egg whites, room temperature	2	(3.9-ounce) packages instant vanilla pudding mix
½	teaspoon water	3½	cups half-and-half
¼	teaspoon salt	½	cup cream
¼	teaspoon cream of tartar	1	cup blueberries
¾	cup sugar	1	cup chopped strawberries
½	cup finely chopped pecans	1	cup sliced peaches
½	teaspoon vanilla		

Preheat the oven to 300 degrees. Beat egg whites and water until foamy. Add salt and cream of tartar and beat until mixture stands in soft peaks. Add sugar gradually while beating, until mixture is very stiff. Fold in nuts and vanilla. Spoon onto non-stick lined baking sheet forming a nest-like shell, making sure to build up sides to form a rim. Bake for 50 to 55 minutes. Cool. Beat half-and-half, cream and vanilla pudding mix. Cool. Pour into meringue shell and chill. Top with fruits.

The recipe allows for originality; you can choose the fruit you like and decorate however you like.

Incredible Chocolate Pudding

2   cups bittersweet chocolate, chopped
2   cups heavy whipping cream,
     divided

3   egg yolks, beaten
1   teaspoon vanilla
½   teaspoon salt

In microwave heat 1 cup whipping cream to a boil ;add chocolate. Set aside. Heat 1 cup whipping cream in heavy gauge saucepan until bubbles appear around the edge of pan and cream is just about to boil. Remove from heat. Gradually whisk in ¼ cup of cream into yolks. Then pour egg-cream mixture into the warm cream and stir well. Add chocolate. Pour into ramekins and chill.

Lemon Custard Phyllo Cups

½ cup sugar
2 tablespoons cornstarch
⅛ teaspoon salt
1 cup cold water
¼ cup fresh lemon juice

1 large egg
½ teaspoon grated lemon peel
2 tablespoons butter, divided
4 sheets phyllo
1 tablespoon sugar

For the custard whisk sugar, cornstarch and salt in a 4-cup glass mixing bowl. Gradually whisk in 1 cup cold water and lemon juice. Whisk until sugar and cornstarch dissolve. Whisk in egg and lemon peel. Add butter. Place in microwave and heat for 2 minutes; stir. You are going to heat for another minute and stir until mixture comes to a boil and continues to repeat at 1 minute intervals until mixture thickens, about 5 minutes. Press plastic wrap onto the surface of the custard and cool to room temperature. Preheat oven to 375 degrees. Stack 4 phyllo sheets onto work surface. Cut phyllo stack into six 4-inch squares. Press 1 phyllo square into each muffin cup (cover remaining phyllo with plastic wrap and damp towel). Using pastry brush, lightly brush with melted butter.

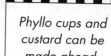

Phyllo cups and custard can be made ahead. Cups should be stored in airtight container and custard needs to be refrigerated.

Press another phyllo square on top of first phyllo square with corners at different angles. Brush with butter. Top with a third phyllo square with corners at different angles. Sprinkle phyllo cups with sugar. Bake until phyllo is golden brown, about 6 minutes. Transfer pan to rack and cook cups completely in pan. Fill with custard.

If time is an issue you can make the cups and buy lemon curd from the grocery but remember homemade is always better.

Lime Sherbet Dessert

1½ cups Ritz cracker crumbs
¼ cup sugar
4 tablespoons butter, melted
1 (2-quart) carton vanilla ice cream

1 (1-quart) carton lime sherbet
¼ cup fresh squeezed lime juice
1 (16-ounce) non-dairy whipped topping

Mix cracker crumbs with sugar and butter until crumbly. Press into a 9x13x2-inch pan. Soften and mix together the vanilla ice cream, lime sherbet and juice. Pour over crust and put in the freezer. Spread whipped topping over the ice cream and place into the freezer.

Mom's Apple Bars

3 cups flour
1 cup shortening
1 egg
⅔ cup milk
1 teaspoon salt
1 teaspoon brown sugar

4 cups apples, peeled and thinly sliced apples
¼ cup cornflakes, crushed
⅔ cup sugar
½ teaspoon cinnamon

Preheat the oven to 375 degrees. Cut shortening into flour and mix egg and milk together and stir into shortening mixture. Roll out half of dough to fit into a ¼ sheet cake pan. Add apples and sprinkle with cornflakes, sugar and cinnamon. Roll remaining dough and place on apples. Bake 40 minutes. Cool and frost with powdered sugar frosting.

This is my mother, Marlene's recipe; she is an amazing cook. One thing I have realized by putting this book together is how much she has influenced who I am as a person.

I have always loved to prepare my mother's recipes but my son always says Grandma's is better. One day I made him French toast as I do often, but this time I put it onto one of my mothers' dinner plates. My son asked what I had done different. I of course said nothing but his comment was, "maybe we should get all of grandma's plates."

Nutty Upside-Down Coffee Cake

1 cup chopped nuts	½ cup milk
½ cup corn syrup	1 teaspoon vanilla
2 tablespoons butter, softened	½ teaspoon ground cinnamon
2 cups baking mix	1 egg
½ cup sugar	

Mix nuts, corn syrup, and butter in a 2-quart baking dish. Spread to cover bottom of pan. Mix remaining ingredients and beat 30 seconds. Spread over pecan mixture. Bake until golden brown and wooden pick inserted in center comes out clean, about 30 minutes. Cool 10 minutes. Invert on heatproof serving plate.

This recipe really should go into a non-stick flexible mold or do the directions in reverse. I love to make this coffee cake in the mold because no one has ever seen one come out of a pan this beautiful before.

Orange Angel Food Cake Roll

1 step Angel Food cake mix	½ cup water
¾ cup frozen Florida orange juice concentrate, thawed	½ cup plain citrus flavored yogurt

Whip Angel Food cake mix with orange juice and water. Pour onto ½ sheet pan lined with non-stick liner; bake 15 minutes. Cool completely. Loose edges with kitchen knife; invert onto non-stick surface and fill with yogurt. Roll like a jelly roll.

Make a lemon Angel Food by replacing lemonade for orange juice and adding a ½ teaspoon lemon peel. Fill with lemon curd.

Pumpkin Cake

1 yellow or white cake mix
1 (10-ounce) can pumpkin
1¼ cups water
3 eggs

2 tablespoons pumpkin pie spice
2 cups white chocolate, chopped
2 cups heavy whipping cream, divided

Preheat the oven to 325 degrees. Mix cake, pumpkin, water, eggs and pumpkin pie spice together. Pour into two 8-inch round pans or a 3-quart baking dish. Bake for 45 to 50 minutes. Cool completely. Slice into 4 layers. For frosting heat 1 cup heavy cream in microwave to boil for 2 minutes add chocolate. Cool frosting at least 3 hours. Whip 1 cup heavy cream about 3 minutes to soft peaks. Fold white chocolate mixture into cream carefully. Frost the cake layers. Place chopped pecans on the sides.

This recipe has a long history. My friend Alicia and I made it for the holidays one year and fell in love with it and then lost the recipe and could not remember how we had made it. Two years later I was visiting with another friend and she was asking me questions about how to make this cake I had once brought to work. As she was talking I realized she was talking about the missing recipe. She made it and brought the recipe to work for me to copy. Alicia was thrilled and so was I.

Pumpkin Custards

1 cup heavy cream	½ teaspoon cinnamon
¾ cup whole milk	1 teaspoon vanilla
¾ cup pure maple syrup	⅛ teaspoon nutmeg, freshly grated
½ cup canned solid-pack pumpkin	¼ teaspoon salt
7 large egg yolks	1 cup whipping cream, whipped

Preheat the oven to 325 degrees. Whisk together cream, milk, syrup, and pumpkin in heavy saucepan and bring to a simmer over moderate heat. Whisk together yolks, cinnamon, nutmeg, vanilla and salt in a bowl. Add hot pumpkin mixture to yolks in a slow stream, whisking constantly. Pour custard through a fine mesh sieve into a large measuring cup and divide among ramekins. Bake custard in a hot water bath for 35 to 40 minutes, covered tightly with foil. Test by inserting a toothpick into the center of custard. It should come out clean. Transfer custards to a rack to cool completely. Chill covered, for at least 2 hours. Whip cream and top custards.

I make these in my non-stick muffin molds and then unmold onto plate and garnish with whipped cream—very elegant. Check out my website for more information on this great product at sheilaraellc.com.

Pumpkin Pie

1 (10-ounce) can packed pumpkin	1 teaspoon cinnamon
3 eggs	¼ teaspoon nutmeg
1 cup brown sugar	1 cup evaporated milk
½ teaspoon salt	1 (9-inch) pie crust

Preheat the oven to 350 degrees. Mix pumpkin, sugar, salt, cinnamon, nutmeg and milk together. Pour into unbaked crust and bake for 1 hour or until knife comes out clean.

Raspberry Cream Pie

4	cups raspberries, divided	½	pint heavy cream
1	cup sugar	1	teaspoon vanilla
1⅓	cups water, divided	1	(9-inch) pie shell, baked
3	tablespoons cornstarch		

In microwave safe bowl heat 1 cup raspberries and 1 cup water for 8 minutes. Mix remaining ⅓ cup water with cornstarch; add to cooked raspberries. Cook until thick, stirring constantly and cool. Add uncooked raspberries. Cool. Pour into pie shell. Whip cream and add vanilla. Pour onto raspberry filling. Chill in refrigerator 3 to 4 hours.

Rhubarb Frozen Yogurt Torte

¾	cup water, divided	3	cups vanilla low fat yogurt
2	teaspoons unflavored gelatin	12	vanilla sandwich cookies, finely chopped
4	cups sliced fresh rhubarb stalks or thawed frozen rhubarb	¼	cup butter, melted
⅔	cup sugar, divided	1	pound strawberries

Put ¼ cup water in a small cup and sprinkle gelatin on top and let gelatin soften while cooking rhubarb. Cook rhubarb with ½ cup sugar and remaining water in a saucepan over moderate heat. Stir occasionally until very soft, about 7 minutes. Add gelatin mixture, stirring until dissolved; cool 10 minutes. Purée in a food processor until smooth, add yogurt and blend well. Refrigerate. While cooling, blend cookie crumbs and butter; spread evenly over bottom of a 2-quart baking dish. Freeze for 20 minutes. Carefully spoon frozen yogurt gently over crumbs and carefully smooth top. Wrap pan in plastic wrap and freeze until firm, overnight. Hull and quarter strawberries, toss with remaining 2 tablespoons sugar, and let stand 15 minutes. Unmold onto serving tray; cut torte into 8 wedges and serve with strawberries.

Rhubarb is wonderful; it grows out of control so just ask your neighbors for some if it is not growing in your yard.

My kids love rhubarb as a drink on a hot summer day; check out the kids section for the recipe.

Rhubarb Refrigerator Dessert

½ cup sugar
3 cups rhubarb, chopped
1 (3-ounce) package strawberry
   gelatin
1 (3.9-ounce) package instant vanilla
   pudding
2 cups milk

1 cup non-dairy whipped topping
2 cups crushed graham crackers
¾ cup plain yogurt
½ teaspoon cinnamon
¼ teaspoon nutmeg

In a saucepan pour sugar over rhubarb; let stand 1 hour. Simmer rhubarb until tender, stirring occasionally. Add gelatin and mix until dissolved. Chill until syrupy. Mix pudding with milk. Fold in non-dairy whipped topping. Add cooled rhubarb. Blend. For crust mix graham crackers, yogurt, cinnamon and nutmeg. Pour ¾ of graham crust into 9x13x2-inch cake pan. Pour rhubarb over graham crust mixture and sprinkle with remaining crust. Refrigerate overnight.

Sheila's Simply Wonderful Cheesecake

2	cups crushed chocolate chip cookies	1	tablespoon vanilla
1/4	cup melted butter	3	eggs, beaten
3	(8-ounce) packages cream cheese	2	cup fresh berries
1	(14-ounce) can sweetened condensed milk		

Preheat the oven to 325 degrees. Mix cookie crumbs and butter. Press into a 2-quart baking dish. Bake 17 minutes. Let cool. Lower the oven temperature to 300 degrees. In a bowl, beat cheese, milk and vanilla until smooth. Add eggs and beat only until incorporated. Pour into crust and bake for 1 hour. Let cool. Remove from pan and serve with fresh berries.

Cheesecakes crack for two reasons:

1. Too hot of oven, which causes the cheesecake to bake too quickly

2. Over mixing creates too much air, which cause the cheesecake to rise too high and then fall as it cools.

I only use molds for this recipe. You can see information on molds at the front of this book or check out the web site at sheilaraellc.com.

1. Stir in ½ cup of mint chocolate chips.

2. Stir in ½ cup of mashed banana and an additional egg yolk.

3. Stir in ½ cup key lime juice and an additional egg yolk.

4. 1 can apple pie filling, 1 teaspoon cinnamon, ¼ cup brown sugar in the bottom of the pan and add cheesecake filling. I do not use a crust on this cheesecake.

Sour Cream Raisin Pie

2	cups sour cream	½	teaspoon salt
1	cup sugar	1	cup raisins
¼	teaspoon nutmeg	4	eggs yolks
¼	teaspoon cinnamon	1	(9-inch) pie crust, baked
5	tablespoons flour		

Preheat the oven to 400 degrees. Combine the sugar, nutmeg, cinnamon, flour and salt. Scald the cream and add the dry ingredients while stirring all the time. Then add the raisins and 4 egg yolks. Pour into crust and cover with meringue. Bake for 12 minutes.

Strawberry Dessert

2	(3-ounce) packages strawberry gelatin	1	(10-ounce) package frozen strawberries, thawed
2	cups hot water	1½	cups heavy whipping cream, whipped
1	cup water	1	Angel Food cake

Dissolve the gelatin in 2 cups hot water and add 1 cup cold water and strawberries. Cool. Fold in whipped cream. Break up cake into small pieces. Pour mixture over cake and toss lightly. Place in 9x13x2-inch pan. Refrigerate 3 hours or overnight.

My mother made this light dessert for our family often. It is absolutely delicious.

Strawberry Pie

2 cups water	3 tablespoons strawberry gelatin
1 cup sugar	4 cups strawberries, cut up
¼ cup cornstarch	1 (9-inch) pie crust, baked

In microwave safe bowl mix water, sugar and cornstarch. Cook 2 minutes and stir; repeat for 8 to 10 minutes. Add gelatin and cool. Add strawberries and pour into a prepared pie crust.

Strawberry Pineapple Pie

½ cup sugar	½ cup corn syrup
¼ cup cornstarch	1½ tablespoons cornstarch
½ teaspoon salt	1 tablespoon water
2½ cups crushed pineapple	1 teaspoon lemon juice
2 tablespoons butter	2 drops red food coloring
1 (9-inch) pie shell, baked	
2 cups strawberries, cut in half, divided	

In microwave safe bowl combine sugar, cornstarch and salt. Drain syrup from pineapple into measuring cup. Add enough hot water to make 1⅔ cups; add to sugar mixture. Cook in microwave for 7 minutes, stirring every minute. Add pineapple and butter and stir until butter melts. Cool and pour into baked pie shell. Arrange larger berries on top of pineapple filling and reserve ½ for the glaze. For the strawberry glaze mash ⅔ cup strawberries and light corn syrup. Cook in the microwave until berries are soft. Mix the cornstarch with water and add to strawberry syrup. Cook until thick, stirring constantly. Add lemon juice and red food coloring. Cool slightly before pouring on pie.

Super Chocolate Cheesecake

½ cup pecans, finely ground	1 cup sour cream
1 cup chocolate cookie crumbs	1 cup sugar
6 tablespoons butter, melted	3 eggs, beaten
2 tablespoons brown sugar	1 cup semi-sweet chocolate, divided
3 (8-ounce) packages cream cheese at room temperature	2 tablespoons vanilla
	¼ cup sour cream

To make crust, combine pecans, cookies, butter and brown sugar; blend well. Press the crumb mixture evenly on bottom and partway up the sides of a 2-quart spring form pan. Chill the crust while preparing the filling. To make the filling, beat cream cheese, sour cream and sugar. Melt ¾ cup chocolate in microwave on 20% power until melted; add vanilla. Add to cream cheese mixture. Add eggs until blended; do not over mix. Pour mixture into prepared pan and bake at 300 degrees for one hour in a water bath. Turn off oven and let cake cool with oven door open. When cake has cooled heat sour cream in microwave for 1 minute and add ¼ cup chocolate. Spread on top of cake. Cool overnight.

Tar Heel Pie

1 cup chocolate chips	½ cup flour
½ cup butter	1 cup brown sugar
1 cup chopped walnuts	2 eggs
1 teaspoon vanilla	1 (9-inch) pie crust, unbaked

Preheat the oven to 350 degrees. Heat butter in the microwave for 1 minute; pour over chocolate chips and stir. Blend all remaining ingredients and stir into chocolate chip mixture. Pour into unbaked pie shell. Bake for 30 to 40 minutes.

This is the easiest pie I have ever made.

Volcano Chocolate Cakes

⅔ cup semi-sweet chocolate, chopped
¾ cup butter
3 large eggs

3 large egg yolks
1½ cups powdered sugar
½ cup all-purpose flour

Heat butter in microwave for 2 minutes. Add chocolate; stir until smooth. Cool slightly. Whisk eggs and egg yolks into chocolate. Stir sugar and flour together and whisk into chocolate mixture. Refrigerate at least 30 minutes, but can be made the day ahead. Preheat oven at 425 degrees. Pour batter into non-stick muffin tray. Bake cakes until sides are set but center remains soft and runny, about 14 minutes. Cool 5 minutes.

This recipe is wonderful. I prefer non-stick muffin molds because they are flexible and allow for easy removal.

INDEX

INDEX

**For ordering information
go to
Sheilaraellc.com**